MW01126035

Since I am a publisher, for 37 years I have consistently followed a self-imposed rule—I would not endorse books from another publisher because it seemed to put me in a conflict of interest situation. But so great is my respect, appreciation, and love for Dennis Kinlaw and his message that, conflict of interest or not, I am breaking that rule and commending this collection of Dennis Kinlaw's sermons to people who wouldn't normally read a book of sermons. I once told Dennis that just observing his life and words almost persuaded me that perhaps the Wesleyan message was on target. He just smiled. These sermons took me back to that conversation and my times of fellowship with him. The sermons in this collection are carefully crafted masterpieces and reveal him as a gifted speaker, writer, and story teller—stories that hold one's interest and make a real point. But more than that, these sermons reveal Dennis's passion for the Wesleyan Holiness message that so characterized his own life and ministry. It is a message that will touch your heart and conscience as it did mine.

Stanley N. Gundry
Senior Vice President and Publisher
Zondervan

It is a distinct honor and a real joy to welcome this collection of some of Dr. Dennis Kinlaw's best-loved sermons and to recommend them to others who value the power and the joy that comes from hearing and reading God's word together. Dennis was a true servant of our Lord who lived and preached in a way that modelled what those same Scriptures taught. Dennis and I were at Brandeis University, Massachusetts, together while he simultaneously carried on a fruitful preaching ministry to New York. I highly commend Dennis's work to all who want to know and serve their Lord better and to follow in the footsteps of a spiritual giant for Christ.

Walter C. Kaiser, Jr., PhD
President Emeritus
Gordon-Conwell Theological Seminary

Here are messages that probe the depths of divine love by one of the giant holiness statesmen of our generation. Dr. Kinlaw's profound insights to Scripture woven into his own experience speak to both the mind and spirit. Uplifting and challenging reading indeed. Take it as a tonic for your soul.

Robert E. Coleman, PhD
Distinguished Senior Professor of Evangelism and Discipleship
Gordon-Conwell Theological Seminary

This delightful collection of sermons is a joyful reminder to all of us why we loved being around Dennis Kinlaw. These sermons capture his theological depth, his wit, and, most of all, his love for Jesus Christ and the glorious gospel! The added bonus of the beautiful and heart-warming introductions by his granddaughter, Cricket Albertson, make this book a real treasure. I heartily recommend it!

Timothy C. Tennent, PhD
President
Asbury Theological Seminary

Dennis Kinlaw preached like Michelangelo painted. Using the pigments of the Scripture and the brush strokes of the Holy Spirit, he created magnificent portraits of the relationship God desires with me—and you. His masterful sermons will grow your faith, deepen your surrender, and leave you in awe of your Father's love.

David Stephens, MD, M.A. (Ethics)
Chief Executive Officer
Christian Medical & Dental Associations

Malchus' Ear

AND
OTHER
SERMONS

OTHER TITLES BY DENNIS F. KINLAW

Preaching in the Spirit (1985)

Song of Songs: Expositor's Bible Commentary (1991)

The Mind of Christ (1998)

We Live as Christ (2001)

This Day with the Master (2002)

Let's Start with Jesus (2005)

Lectures in Old Testament Theology (2010)

Prayer: Bearing the World (2013)

Malchus' Ear

AND OTHER SERMONS

Dennis F. Kinlaw

EDITED BY CRICKET ALBERTSON

Francis Asbury Press
Wilmore, Kentucky

Francis Asbury Society

PO Box 7
Wilmore, KY 40390
859-858-4222
800-530-5673
fas@francisasburysociety.com
www.francisasburysociety.com

ISBN 978-0-915143-30-6
Cover design by Kaiser Shaffer
Printed in the United States of America

In Loving Memory of

Mickey Marvin

Friend of Jesus

"For to me, to live is Christ and to die is gain." (Philippians 1:21)

Contents

Foreword

Almost twenty years ago, I found myself working as a secretary at Asbury College (now Asbury University). I had graduated the previous year and was working to help my new husband finish school. I quickly realized that after the rigor of college life, being a secretary proved rather tedious, and I wanted something to think about while I typed and copied. I enrolled across the street at Asbury Theological Seminary in a course on C. S. Lewis taught by Jerry Walls. That class became a catalyst for a whole new world for me. I enrolled full time at the seminary and studied church history, philosophy, and theology. As I approached graduation, I was offered the position of theological assistant to my grandfather, Dennis Kinlaw. My job was to assist him in writing projects and to help him in any way I could.

My theological journey with Papa began in this way. I came to work for him as an assistant, and instantly he handed me books to read that I had never read before: John MacMurray, Colin Gunton, and Thomas Torrance were the first ones to come my way. I would read, and then we would meet to talk them over, and my theological training grew by leaps and bounds. I had signed up to help Papa and found my own spiritual world was being transformed. Seminary provided the foundation, but my conversations with Papa catapulted me into a whole new spiritual, theological, and philosophical world. Knowing Jesus was, for Papa, the key to life, and I found that I knew Jesus more because of my time spent with Papa in serious intellectual discussions. I could not get enough. Even when I became a mom we continued to work together. I would stick theology books in my diaper bags, and off we would go to see Papa.

Papa was thrilled to have a young mind to train, and I was thrilled to spend my time learning from him and helping him. I began listening to Papa's sermons on my drives to work, and I realized that they would provide perfect material for a daily devotional book. I listened to hundreds of sermons, and from those drives a devotional book taken from Papa's sermons and chapel talks, *This Day with the Master*, came into existence. Later, Papa's theological treatise, *Let's Start with Jesus*, and his book, *Prayer: Bearing the World*, were published.

In 2012, Papa's health suffered a serious decline. On April 4, we were faced with a medical emergency, and so we quickly moved Papa into our home so we could care for him. This began a season of joy for my family; my husband and my three children found that life grew better in every way with Papa in the front room. For the next five years, Papa's presence filled our daily life with Jesus' love. For the first few years, Papa and I continued to do all the theological work we could do together. Then Papa became more frail, and my job became one of caregiving instead of assisting, but in those last years Papa was ever teaching me about Jesus, his love, his provision, and his care. I found Psalm 23:6 to be true. The goodness and love of God followed Papa all the days of his life, and we lived in that goodness and love because Papa lived in our home.

For a long time, I have wanted to put together a book of Papa's sermons. Like John Wesley, Papa was known for his preaching more than his works of theology. In preaching, he could make theological and biblical truths accessible to every believer, from the child to the most academically trained. These sermons represent some of the most intellectually and spiritually pivotal insights of Papa's life. They are hallmarks of his faith and of his understanding of the gospel. Before each sermon, I have included a brief introduction to give the reader a context for the sermon in Papa's thinking and experience. All of these sermons come from Papa's personal encounter with Christ; therefore, it seemed important to include Papa's own testimony as the first chapter in this book. He wrote this testimony in the last five years of his life as he remembered God's goodness to him throughout his life. This testimony sets the stage for all the sermons that follow. Papa believed that a personal encounter with Christ was the key to all intellectual and spiritual discovery.

—Cricket Albertson

The Personal Testimony of Dennis F. Kinlaw

A person in his nineties has a good bit to remember; for one thing, he has just been around for a long time. Another factor, perhaps even more significant, is that he has more free time on his hands to remember. That has surely been true for me. A third point that haunts me is the question of whether I owe it to my present and future family to leave a witness of the great mercies of God that in his goodness he has given to our family. It is this last one that moves me at the moment.

As I look back across my life and that of my family, it is not difficult for me to see the hand of God in it from the very beginning. I attribute this to the Christian character of my parents from before my birth. I was born into a devout home with a mother and a father who shared a remarkable hunger to know God and to serve him. My mother was a schoolteacher before she married my father. He also had been a teacher who decided to go to law school and become a lawyer. We were Methodists and had one treasured volume of John Wesley's sermons in our home in the 1920s, along with other good Christian books like *The Christ of the Indian Road* by E. Stanley Jones. The most important book in our home, though, was the Bible, which both my father and my mother read daily.

As I said, we were Methodists. More important for us, though, was the fact that evangelists were a part of our culture. They came from time to time for evangelistic crusades that were held in such neutral places as the court house, one of the public markets used for tobacco sales in season, or even a tent that the evangelist would bring with him. These were normally interdenominational and provided something that our Baptist, Presbyterian, Episcopalian, Methodist, or Christian and Missionary Alliance churches could not seem to give. It was through these evangelistic crusades that my father and mother came to an immediate and genuine personal knowledge of the living Christ that was more intense and fulfilling than that which they had found just through the regular life in the Church. After such an introduction to Christ, the greatest passion of my parents was that the children that God had given them would know God in a real and authentic way. So, my father and mother had an intense interest in exposing us to the godliest of persons that they could find. They did not leave that burden to anyone else; they assumed it as their primary obligation. An example of how deeply they felt it occurred before I was ten years of age and occurred in such a way that its impact on me could not be removed or forgotten.

Those were Depression days. One day, my father came home from his office in the late afternoon and said to my mother, "Sally, our bank closed today and we have lost all of our savings." He changed his clothes to go to work in one of our two gardens, which kept us alive during those days, singing as he went: "Be not dismayed whate'er betide, God will take care of you."

Some of the kids in my class had a few cents of their own and at recess time would buy chocolate Tootsie Rolls for a penny a piece. I found myself envying them and wishing that I had a little money, too. One morning, I rose a bit early, dressed for school, and then slipped into the room where my mother kept her purse, opened it, found a dollar bill, which I took, and then went for a walk. After a brief walk, I returned to show my mother my dollar bill and told her that I had found it while I was out. My mother finished the breakfast she was preparing for me and for my older brother and sister.

As we ate, my mother turned to us and informed us that she realized that I was not feeling very good and she had decided to let me stay home that day from school. I instantly felt sick; in our family, there was almost nothing important enough to keep one from going to school. My brother and sister left, and I went into the family room and sat down to face what was coming. Mother finished her dishes and then came in and pulled up her chair next to mine. In the gentlest tone, she told me that she knew that I had not found the dollar on my walk but had taken it from her purse. Then she expressed her regret that we did not have enough money to give me some of my own on occasion, but she explained the difficulties that we were living with financially as a family.

Then she turned to me, with her eyes brimming a bit, and said, "But what hurts me the most, Honey, is not that you would deceive me, but that you today have grieved the heart of the One who loves you the most: Jesus." It was years later that I remembered this incident and realized that she had said nothing about my doing wrong by breaking the moral law or making God angry. The primary problem here was not legal but *personal*. I had grieved the very *Person* whom I should recognize as the best of all possible friends, the One from whom I had received the most and to whom I owed the most.

I know now that she was infinitely smarter than she knew she was. She knew things about reality and was able to think thoughts intellectually that no Greek philosopher had ever been able to know or think. To think of persons as *persons* and human relationships as personal was as natural for her as to look upon gravity as a reality that no one could escape. And all of this had come out of her personal relationship with Christ and her submersion of herself into the thought world of the Scriptures. She would have been shocked to learn that the terminology that was to be used to express the simple concept of personhood was not developed until the Council of Chalcedon in A.D. 451 and that the word *person* itself and the truth it expressed was the gift of the Church at that time to the world, though the world did not recognize it. The first human being to be identified as a *person* was Jesus himself. She probably would not have been as shocked as I was when I learned all of this in my early eighties and realized that, in a lifetime in academic studies in theology, philosophy, biblical studies, psychology, and sociology, no professor had ever discussed this unbelievably important contribution of Christ and the Scriptures with me.

Slowly, as the years passed, I realized that she was, without knowing it, the first and greatest teacher of metaphysics that I was to have. She had begun to introduce me to the nature of the ultimate absolute of all absolutes that lies behind all things. According to her, that from which we come is not primarily a power, a metaphysical principle, a moral law, or a concept but One who, as a divine personal being, has visited us in personal human form through a personal birth, a personal life, a personal death, and a personal resurrection and ascension back to the divine personal interrelationships that he had left. The first chapter of the book of Genesis tells us this truth: when man was created, he was made in the very *image* and *likeness* of God, the personal One.

My mother was telling me that I was not, as Plato thought, the product of an impersonal world of truth, goodness, and beauty, nor, as Aristotle would think, a rational animal, the product of an Uncaused Cause or Unmoved Prime Mover. I was a human person and had offended a living divine Person who was actually the friend of all possible friends. I was made in his image and was a *person*, too. She was pushing me into a totally new world—that world of persons, human and divine, that only Christians really know. I am quite confident that she did not know the creative nature of the philosophical concepts implicit in her handling of me. I have learned, though, that it is possible to know realities sometimes that you do not even know that you know. Time has let me know that this is one of the major advantages that comes from submersion of one's mind in the Scriptures.

Recognizing Jesus as the One whom we all must encounter was the first step in my coming to know Christ. The second step came in a most unusual way—out of my father's morning prayer meeting in the courthouse. One of my father's friends who attended this morning prayer meeting made a good bit of his income by selling citrus fruit on Saturdays in the farmer's market. One day, the conversation turned to the fact that Billy Sunday was coming to western North Carolina to preach in a men's conference. My father's friend told the group that he wanted to go hear Sunday. He invited my father to go with him.

God had put in my father's heart a deep and passionate love for the preaching of the gospel. He took every opportunity to hear good preachers, so he decided to go and hear Billy Sunday. The two men traveled some two hundred miles in the midst of the Depression in the cab of an old fruit truck to hear the gospel preached. When God puts that kind of hunger in a man's heart to hear the gospel, you should watch closely. It usually means that God is up to something—and he was!

After they had heard Sunday preach, my father's friend said, "Wade, I need a load of fruit. Let's go home by way of Florida." So, my father found himself starting on a long trip, which he did not want to take, in the cab of that old truck.

When they got to Georgia, they found themselves passing Indian Springs Holiness Camp Meeting. In the providence of God, though they never planned it, they found themselves passing this camp meeting when it was actually in session, which only happens ten days each year. My father said, "Let's stop and see what this is." They did. They heard Henry Clay Morrison, the president of Asbury College and the founder of Asbury Theological Seminary, preach. My father said to his friend, "You go on to Florida and pick me up on your way back." He did just that, and only eternity can reveal the results for the kingdom of God. Don't underestimate the creativity of God. When my father got home, he said to my mother, "Sally, we have to take the kids." Our world had changed.

Two years later, as a boy of thirteen, I found myself on my way, quite unwillingly, to Georgia to attend a holiness camp meeting where, to my horror, I had learned that I would be attending two youth and three preaching services every day for ten days. For me, that was quite an unhappy prospect.

The first session each day was a Bible class for teenage boys. It was taught by an older lady whose calling in life was to teach young boys as they entered their teens. She was affectionately called Mother Clark. She knew and understood her charges. She began to teach about sin and salvation, and she did it in such a way that we could not misunderstand.

She cleverly took a piece of red construction paper and cut out of its center a large heart. She then glued a piece of white paper to the back of the red construction sheet so that now the open heart appeared quite white and clean. She explained that Jesus wanted us to have clean white hearts like the heart in the construction paper frame. Her question was, "Is your heart white like this one?" I was quite glad that she could not see my heart!

Then she reached for a large flashlight that she always carried with her. She turned it on and put it behind the white heart. Suddenly, that heart was not spotless. Black spots took shape in the white sheet that she was showing us. The white sheet behind the red construction sheet was not a single sheet. It was two sheets glued together, and small black pieces of paper had been glued between the white sheets. She explained that Jesus, through the Holy Spirit, can look into our hearts and see what no one else can see. I suddenly felt exposed with no place to hide. Mother Clark simply watched me. On the third day, she said to me, "Dennis, will you help me after class carry my things back to the hotel?" I was quite flattered.

I have always loved her wisdom. When the rest of the class had gone, she turned to me and asked, "Dennis, have you ever let Jesus cleanse your heart?" She did not ask me if I had been baptized or if I had joined the Church. I had already taken care of those issues. She had me back to the Jesus thing. I have often, in recalling this moment, thought that had it been my mother or my Sunday school teacher who had been asking this I would have lied. I found, though, that I was in a different atmosphere, confronted by one who clearly loved me and could care for a thirteen-year-old boy. Actually, a lie was unthinkable in that context. In stumbling speech, I confessed my "No." When she suggested that we pray to ask Christ to forgive me, it seemed the most right thing we could possibly do.

Suddenly, Christ was no longer a distant figure to fear but the friend of all possible friends. That night, as I said my prayers before slipping into bed, I lovingly, earnestly, and ignorantly assured Jesus that I would never sin against him again. I had slipped into a new world, and I was made new.

Three nights later, I found myself sitting with Mother Clark, a new friend that was my age, named Buddy Luce, and some other young people in the evening preaching service. Henry Clay Morrison, the president of Asbury College and Seminary, a famous evangelist, and the one whom my father had heard when he had discovered the camp meeting, was the preacher. His subject was personal holiness. He used language that was new and strange to me, but the burden of his message was quite clear to my thirteen-year-old mind. He told us how Christ loved us, wanted to be very close to us. He told us how Christ wanted to belong to us and wanted us to belong completely to him. I found my heart flooded with a surprising love and with a profound desire to please Jesus. It seemed as natural now to run to him as it would have been before that week to avoid him if possible. I found myself joyfully kneeling at the altar eager to let him know that I wanted to be wholly his.

In the years since, I have never found words adequate to describe to anyone what those next few hours were like. It was years before I even tried. Human language just could not do justice to what occurred. It was a profoundly emotional moment. A joy flooded my inner being, a joy of a deeper magnitude and of a different essence than anything I had ever known before. Later, I found myself thinking of it in terms of the promise in Romans 5:5, that the Holy Spirit can shed abroad in the human heart the very love that binds the three persons of the Holy Trinity together in the human believer's heart. There was a marvelous sense of inner cleanness that now seemed to leave my inner spirit as if it had been cleansed from all of the normal defilements that haunt a thirteen-year-old boy's conscience. Yet even this sense of cleansing was not my primary consciousness. That was completely different. It was the sense of a Presence, an Other, who had come to me. All of the bits of glory of that moment seemed to be the natural accompaniments that came with that holy Presence. It was not just that I felt that he had now entered into me and that I now possessed him. Rather, he had welcomed me into himself. I did not have to reach out to touch him. He was in me, and I was in him. Later, I would learn the Trinitarian language behind the concepts of *"the exchanged life," "co-inherence,"* and *"circumincession,"* but, for that moment, what I felt was that he possessed me, that *I was his and he was mine.*

I was in contact with another world, one that transcends the time to which our clocks bear witness. The night was wearing on. The thought of leaving that holy place never crossed my mind. Finally, my mother came and said, "Son, you need to go to bed." There were two ladies who continued to kneel at the altar although the congregation was long gone. I looked at my mother and said, as I pointed to two ladies who were still kneeling at the altar, "Go home before they have found what I have found?" Such was absolutely unthinkable! I had found the Pearl of Great Price, and I knew that it had to be shared. Somehow, I knew that this was for the whole world, and I must do what I could do so that all might know the One who had now given himself in his fullness to me.

My mother, in an amazing moment of wisdom, left me alone. All that night, I gloried in that Presence in a flow of love that I knew did not have its source in me. That night, I sensed, though I could not fully understand, that he had chosen to love his world and all its inhabitants, that this love is more than something he does—it is who he is—and to dwell in him is to dwell in that love (Rom 5:5, 1 Jn 4:8, 16).

That was the first night in my thirteen-year-old life that I went the whole night without going to sleep. It was six-thirty the next morning during the prayer meeting that I fell sound asleep in my pew!

Needless to say, the intensity of the sense of his presence did not become an unbroken constancy for me. It would have been too much, but he had let me taste. The memory became the foundation stone of my personal existence. I knew that the living Christ was a reality, a reality that could not be denied. I had met him and had known his love.

When I came home after the camp meeting was over, in a moment of confidence with my pastor, I began to tell him that I had met Christ. His response was, "Well, Dennis! You don't think that that has to happen to everyone, do you?" My thirteen-year-old mind reacted in a certain horror at the thought of classifying my encounter with Christ as something I might think *had to* happen to anyone. The possibility of knowing the God that I had found was no longer in a category of duty but one of pure joy without equal. Having come to know God in this intimacy, the thought that this was not available in a world created by him to everyone in the world created by him was just unthinkable—impossible! Without knowing it, I was becoming a Wesleyan and an Asburian.

The immediate impact of the coming of Christ and his Spirit to me was profound. I moved into a new world as far as my consciousness, my knowledge, was concerned. The fact that God actually existed, could be encountered and personally known, was no longer a matter of debate for me. God was no longer an idea, a concept to be thought, or even a dogma to be believed. He was more, and meeting him had changed me. Two life-changing events had occurred. One was intellectual. It manifested itself in a hunger to know, a hunger that had a transforming effect on me and my daily life. So, at thirteen I began to read—and read seriously. The other was more personal. It was the knowledge that there is a fulfillment in his presence that can birth a passion that makes everything in your existence other than secondary. He can become the love of one's life. This may be why Paul tells his friends in Philippi, "For to me, to live is Christ . . ." (Phil 1:21).

The sense of the presence of God in my life continued but with a diminution that caused me to wonder if it would all just become a very unusual memory, but there were moments of renewal. They were not as overwhelming as the original, but I began to realize that they had the same authenticity. I also began to realize something about the knowledge of another person that was different from other kinds of knowledge. It became clear rather quickly that personal relations can never be frozen. I began to realize that friendships can be costly and that they demand time. They also demand a place of meeting.

In our home, we had what in those days was spoken of as a parlor. It was a room specially set apart and furnished so that it could be used for social purposes like funerals, weddings, or the hosting of those important guests that a family might on occasion have to entertain. The result was that it was a room apart and somewhat isolated from normal family traffic. The parlor became my holy place, my place of meeting with the newfound Friend.

When I awakened in the morning, I would slip into the parlor where I could be alone. I would take my Bible. I would lay the Bible in the seat of an overstuffed chair and kneel in front of it. I would later hear the story that told of how Luther said that the Bible was the crib in which we could find "the baby Jesus" if we would seek him there. What I found was that, when I humbly read the text and listened for the Inner Voice, I would not often be disappointed.

That stuffed chair in a stuffy parlor became the central trysting place of my life. It was there, as I knelt before an open Bible, as I opened myself to the text and to the Holy One who came to me through it, that the foundations of my life were laid. It was there that the understanding began to come of what it means under God to be in a living relationship with him.

Needless to say, I learned many things there over those years. As I look back, though, one thing is clear to me. I learned that God will speak to those who listen for his voice. I did not know yet the teaching of the Scripture on this. It was only later that I would become familiar with words of the Old Testament Psalmist and prophets as they described the idols of the nations around Israel and compared them with Israel's own God, Yahweh. The value of an idol is one given to the god by its worshippers. There is one value that the worshippers cannot give: they cannot make them talk. Yahweh, though, is pictured from the Garden as coming to seek his creatures. He comes, and he comes calling. And the final biblical word is God saying "Come!"—"The Spirit and the bride say, 'Come!' and let the one who hears say, 'Come!' Let the one who is thirsty come; and let the one who wishes take the free gift of the water of life" (Rev 22:17). The biblical God talks when we come to him. During those high school years, I began to hear his voice.

There was something so right and so glorious about my encounter with Christ that the thought that everyone would want to know him and enjoy an unbroken relationship, an intimate relationship, with him seemed the most logical thing that one could think. I found that there were very few who had come to know him as I had come to know him. And the ones who had met Christ were few and far between. None of my natural friends could understand and share my joy. When I shared with my closest buddy what had happened, he wept. He looked at me and responded humbly, "Dennis, I want to be good but I just can't!" Part of what made that very moving to me was that he was the best boy, the cleanest and the fairest, that I had ever known. I knew he was a better person than I was. It was not about being good but about knowing Christ and being known by Christ. Our friendship continued, but there was a dimension to my life that we could not share. My experience in church was similar. In the four years of my life in high school, though immersed in the life of my church, I never had the privilege of a conversation with anyone in the church in which it was clear to me that the other person had experienced the kind of immediacy with Christ that had transformed my existence—until my senior year.

In the winter of that senior year, a girl, whose family was active in our church just as my own family was, sought me out to tell me of an unusual experience that she had had at Christmas time. She and her mother were visiting an aunt. In the family fellowship, the aunt shared with them that she was reading through the *Standard Sermons of John Wesley*. She spoke with some excitement about what a blessing they were to her. Remarkably, they decided to make a reading of some of Wesley's sermons part of their family Christmas celebration. For the first time, my friend heard of Wesley's teaching on the witness of the Spirit and an assurance of personal salvation. She began to seek just that. I can never forget the moment when she told me how Christ had come to meet her. We began to share our gleanings from Wesley with each other. The fellowship was rich. We knew it must be shared. We read that Wesley went and shared Christ with prisoners in the jails, so we determined to do the same. I have often smiled thinking about our local jailor and what she thought when she found herself confronted by two teenagers from familiar and reputable families in the town asking for the privilege of sharing with the prisoners the joys of knowing Jesus. She let us in. My ministry began that day, and so did my friend Sarah's. Her later life was spent with our denominational overseas mission program. The happiest part of this for me was that I now knew someone in my context with whom I could share the deepest joy of my life. I had found a friend who knew and loved my Friend. I also found that there was something about Christ, that when you walked with him, he got you out of yourself and made you think of others.

The key to those years for me, the one that made some sense of it all, was the recurrent coming of that presence to grace my teenage life. I use the term "recurrent" purposely. I had discovered the poetry of Ralph Spaulding Cushman. His poem "The Secret" describes my experience of God's presence.

> I met God in the morning
> When the day was at its best,
> And His Presence came like sunrise,
> Like a glory in my breast.
>
> All day long the Presence lingered,
> All day long he stayed with me,
> And we sailed in perfect calmness
> O'er a very troubled sea.
>
> Other ships were blown and battered,
> Other ships were sore distressed,
> But the winds that seemed to drive them
> Brought to us a peace and rest.
>
> Then I thought of other mornings,
> With a keen remorse of mind,

When I too had loosed the moorings,
With the Presence left behind.

So I think I know the secret
Learned from many a troubled way:
You must seek Him in the morning
If you want Him through the day!

The sense of the presence of Christ began to be the anchor point of my existence. It was the source of my deepest joy. And I found that the best part of it all came when I sensed that he was speaking, too.

I slowly began to realize that there were times when I neither heard his voice nor sensed his presence. I found that there was a price attached to intimacy with Christ. I could not presume upon him; I could not take him for granted. Our relationship was a personal relationship, and personal relationships demand time. Both parties must open themselves to each other. There must be conversation. There must be talk, but there must be listening, too. That means that friends must be intimate enough, close enough, that both know the other is paying attention. Friends must listen to each other if the friendship is to be real. In those teen years, with failures as well as successes, I began to intuit all of this in my walk with Christ.

I noticed that there were times when he was closer than at others. I also found that there were places where I sensed his presence more openly. Some of those places were not where I would have naturally chosen to have found him. One such place was the Tabernacle, a nondescript little church outside of town. As I indicated earlier, the Tabernacle did not enjoy the social status of the other churches, and there were clear and obvious reasons. The pastors of the Tabernacle were normally not university or seminary graduates, while the pastors of my Methodist church were normally Duke or even Yale alumni. They were laymen who had attended a Bible school somewhere; often, they were bi-vocational. The larger part of the attendees were not from our town, not to say anything about from "uptown." They were largely from the mill villages that surrounded our town. One would meet few, or none, of the "shakers and movers" in our town there. But, interestingly enough, I found Jesus there, and there was something about finding him there that matched and fitted what I found through the biblical text in that stuffed chair in the parlor. I found I could not live without both places of encounter. I could not leave my Methodist church because of my family, but slowly I began to slip away on Sunday nights to share in worship with fellow believers.

The Tabernacle may have been at the bottom of the social scale in our town, but at that bottom it had an opening on a world that I would never have known about if I had been limited to the world that my Methodist church opened for me. The Tabernacle had an informal relationship with the Christian and Missionary Alliance (C&MA) movement. That meant that I began to learn about A. B. Simpson, the C&MA founder. I began to see, hear, and meet missionaries from across the world. My introduction to A. B. Simpson followed me. He influenced Charles and Lettie Cowman, who led the Oriental Missionary Society on which Board I would eventually serve. I even began attending a Monday afternoon women's missionary prayer meeting at the Tabernacle where I met young ladies, graduates from Nyack Missionary Training Institute, who were on their way to some mission field but were serving in what were called "community houses" in the textile mills around us. I also joined a Friday after-school Bible study where I was carefully introduced to the theology contained in the footnotes of the Scofield Reference Bible, not my final theological destination but an unbelievably helpful step on the way for a liberal Methodist.

The years have taught me that one is ill advised who attempts to find Jesus where one wants him to be. One is much wiser to seek him where he is, for there—and there alone—will one find the door that opens upon the whole world for both time and eternity. In all of this, I began to learn that Jesus does not come by way of Rome and Jerusalem but by way of a stall and a manger and a town from which nothing good ever came (Jn 1:46).

When we look back across the decades, we can see more clearly that "aggressive benevolence" in God toward us. He is not caught in our time succession, so he can see the relationships necessary to prove that he is *Pro Nobis* ("for us," Rom 8:31). All the blessings of my life came out of this encounter with Christ at Indian Springs. He began to weave my life together in ways of richest blessing and joy. He led me to Asbury College where I found a fellowship of likeminded believers. After the lack of Christian fellowship in my hometown, Asbury seemed like heaven itself. It was there, in chapel, that I met missionary kids and heard the stories of God's work around the world. It was at Asbury that I heard a young lady from New York give her testimony of meeting Christ and full surrender. I knew that she knew him like I had come to know him. The next day, I parked myself outside her mailbox, hoping for an introduction. Fifty-nine and a half years of marriage to her was the greatest gift God ever gave me except for himself.

As I look back on the way God ordered my intellectual life and my career in evangelism, in pastoring and in teaching and in administration, I find that he has been good and faithful at every point, opening doors for me of which I never could have even dreamed. Full surrender should not terrify us. He will be to us the Friend of all friends, and his aggressive love will go before us and behind us all the days of our lives. I have known this to be true!

Dennis Kinlaw entered the immediate presence of the Friend of all friends on April 10, 2017. Dennis gave his life to the proclamation of the gospel around the world primarily through preaching and teaching. His love for Christ, his theological vision, and his passion for learning brought encouragement and blessing to the many who heard him. The following sermons express his journey in faith and understanding. The testimony, which precedes the sermons in this book, is one of the last things he wrote; he wrote it as a witness to the goodness and faithfulness of God.

1

Malchus' Ear: God's Last Love Note to Caiaphas

John 18:1-14

Papa was very interested in symbols. He believed that God was the best third grade school teacher because of the object lessons and stories that he uses to communicate eternal and metaphysical truth. Furthermore, Papa believed God was constantly weaving into our lives and into our world witnesses to himself. C. S. Lewis and Charles Williams played key roles in helping Papa think of the way God gives his witness and draws people to himself. Lewis wrote of God's "unscrupulous ways" in drawing men and women to himself. God has no desire to be formulaic but will use any means to draw people to himself. This sermon gives the best illustration of the lengths to which God will go to give a witness to himself.

As Papa began to work on the stories of the cross and the resurrection in order to preach from them, he found that this story was filled with unexpected detail. When he started to put all the details together from the four Gospels, he realized that God had given a remarkable witness to the most powerful man in Jerusalem right before Jesus' trial. Papa never got over the impact of God's persevering love and grace for Caiaphas through the incident with Malchus' ear. Papa began to look for symbolic Malchus' ear incidents in the news, in politics, in culture, and in history. Every story became an opportunity to see God at work, giving people a chance to receive his love and grace. Papa would state that even *The New York Times* gave a witness to Jesus on the front page, the second line of every newspaper they printed: the date. Human history itself has been told in terms of this God-man from Galilee.

This sermon appeals to all generations and has become a favorite for our family. Whenever something occurs in our family, in our community, or in politics that gives a witness to Jesus, someone will rub his ear and say "Malchus' Ear." Even my children, Papa's great-grandchildren, can understand this story on the love of God that reaches out to the most hardened and the most lost. They can easily imagine Malchus' gratitude and wonder and Caiaphas's shock and perplexity after Jesus replaced the piece of Malchus' ear that Peter had sliced off. This story encapsulates Papa's belief in the passionate and pursuing love of God for his whole world and his radical attempts to reach each one.

When he had finished praying, Jesus left with his disciples and crossed the Kidron Valley. On the other side there was a garden, and he and his disciples went into it.

Now Judas, who betrayed him, knew the place, because Jesus had often met there with his disciples. So Judas came to the garden, guiding a detachment of soldiers and some officials from the chief priests and the Pharisees. They were carrying torches, lanterns and weapons.

Jesus, knowing all that was going to happen to him, went out and asked them, "Who is it you want?"

"Jesus of Nazareth," they replied.

"I am he," Jesus said. (And Judas the traitor was standing there with them.) When Jesus said, "I am he," they drew back and fell to the ground.

Again he asked them, "Who is it you want?"

"Jesus of Nazareth," they said.

Jesus answered, "I told you that I am he. If you are looking for me, then let these men go." This happened so that the words he had spoken would be fulfilled: "I have not lost one of those you gave me."

Then Simon Peter, who had a sword, drew it and struck the high priest's servant, cutting off his right ear. (The servant's name was Malchus.)

Jesus commanded Peter, "Put your sword away! Shall I not drink the cup the Father has given me?"

Then the detachment of soldiers with its commander and the Jewish officials arrested Jesus. They bound him and brought him first to Annas, who was the father-in-law of Caiaphas, the high priest that year. Caiaphas was the one who had advised the Jewish leaders that it would be good if one man died for the people. (John 18:1–14)

The account of Jesus' arrest is obviously essential to the crucifixion story, but the way John the Evangelist handles this story indicates its importance within the larger story. John is the only Gospel writer who does not write about Jesus' Gethsemane experience but he records the arrest of Jesus in remarkable detail. All four evangelists record this story, each one with a different emphasis, adding to the details that we know about Jesus' arrest.

John describes all the people who assembled in the Garden of Gethsemane that night. Jesus is there with his eleven disciples, and then the traitor Judas arrives with a crowd of people: the Roman soldiers, the high priest's servants, the Pharisees, and the temple scribes. The story even describes a young man lingering on the outskirts wearing only a loincloth. Tradition has it that this man is John Mark. All of these different parties come together in this one story; a combination of Jewish authority and Roman authority have come to the garden to seize Jesus. Jesus is identified for them by Judas, although certainly many of them must have known him; they had heard him in the temple that week, and they had been observing him for the last three years.

Judas approaches Jesus and identifies him with a kiss, a stark contrast to the crowd that has come to arrest him carrying torches and weapons as if he were a dangerous criminal. The soldiers undoubtedly have a certain amount of fear in their own hearts: they know that Jesus will have eleven men with him, and they could easily cause problems and try to prevent Jesus' arrest. The soldiers come prepared to seize a violent man and subdue his followers.

Jesus knows what is about to happen and goes forward to them and asks them, "Who is it that you want?"

"Jesus of Nazareth," they reply.

"I am he," Jesus answers.

The Greek simply says, "I AM," which is the name of the God of Israel given to Moses in the book of Exodus (Ex 3:14). When the soldiers and the officers hear this declaration, they step back and fall to the ground. Some commentators argue that the soldiers are simply paying respect to a deity. I highly doubt that; they have come to arrest Jesus with a certain amount of apprehension, and, instead of a revolt, he simply steps forward and gives himself up to them even as he declares his own deity. Jesus is fully in control at that moment, and they are struck with amazement and fall to the ground. The presence of Christ has something so supernatural about it that they are more afraid of him, by far, than he is of them. They hesitate, and he asks again: "Who is it you want?"

"Jesus of Nazareth," they say.

Jesus answers, "I told you that I am he. If you are looking for me, then let these men go."

Jesus has been in the temple that entire week. These men have seen him in broad daylight and could have arrested him at any time, but, probably because they are afraid the crowds would fight for Jesus, they wait until the odds are in their favor. They come at night, with soldiers and torches and swords, to capture him. Instead of the struggle they came prepared for, Jesus simply surrenders himself to them and requests that his friends go free. Jesus willingly surrenders, but the soldiers bind him with ropes to secure him. Obviously, they do not know what to do with this man. This arrest is unlike anything they have ever done before. Perhaps they think that if Jesus is handcuffed there will be no more surprises on this fateful night. I am sure it seemed easier to handle a handcuffed man than the Son of God.

As the soldiers bind Jesus' hands and feet, Peter watches, and all the hopes that he has cherished over the past three years vanish—at least, all hope he ever had of an earthly kingdom. Earlier this very night, Peter had pledged his loyalty to Jesus, whether to live or to die. He had declared, "I will lay down my life for you" (Jn 13:37), and now he stands by while Jesus is bound by Roman ropes. In desperation, Peter decides to fight, and he reaches for one of the two swords the disciples have brought with them. He swings wildly and cuts off a man's ear. The reader's sympathies are more with Peter than the man who lost his ear. Peter means to defend Jesus and start the revolution, but all he does is snip off part of a servant's ear.

One of the surprising things about this story is that all four evangelists record details about this man who loses his ear. All four state that he is the servant of the *high priest*. All four Gospels state that he is *the* servant of the high priest; this means that this servant holds a strategic and influential position as the high priest's assistant. It may also indicate how concerned the high priest is about this arrest that he sends his particular servant to make sure that all goes well. It is this man whose earlobe Peter slices.

We also know that Peter cut off the servant's right ear and not his left ear. That creates some interesting problems. How does a right-handed fellow with a sword catch a right-handed guy across from him in the right ear? Some people suggest that Peter is left-handed or that he attacks from behind. I think it simply reflects the dismay and the consternation that Peter feels at that moment. He is probably aiming for the servant's neck and just takes off part of his ear. The Greek indicates that Peter hit not his whole ear but the lobe of his right ear.

The writers also record this servant's personal name. His name is Malchus. Think of all the people in the Scriptures whose names we do not know, but the Holy Spirit for some reason gives to us the name of the high priest's servant. His name is perpetuated because he is cut by the sword of Peter as he desperately tries to protect Jesus.

Immediately, Jesus says, "Put your sword away! Shall I not drink the cup the Father has given me?" (Jn 18:11). Jesus turns and touches

Malchus' ear, and he is healed (Lk 22:51). Jesus gives himself over to the soldiers, and the soldiers release the disciples just as Jesus has asked, even though one of them has just pulled out a sword. Then they lead Jesus away for his trial.

Jesus has absolute mastery in this moment. I have the suspicion that his pulse is the steadiest and slowest one there. The soldiers obviously have been brought in because the temple authorities needed help. The temple authorities are too nervous to arrest Jesus during the day, so they are doing it in the night when the crowd will not see them. There is apprehension in the Romans and the temple guards and confusion in the hearts and the minds of the disciples. No one knows what is taking place except Jesus himself, but the others know enough to know that it is beyond their knowledge and ability. Peter's act of aggression becomes a symbol of all the confusion and uncertainty.

Jesus is the only one who is in complete control of the situation. Matthew adds to the scene to make Jesus' power even more evident, "Do you think I cannot call on my Father, and he will at once put at my disposal more than twelve legions of angels? But how then would the Scriptures be fulfilled that say it must happen in this way?" (Matt 26:53–54). Jesus understands everything that is taking place at that moment as within the sovereign will, the overarching purposes and the redemptive intentions, of his Father involved in the salvation of the world. So why should Jesus fight it? He does not resist. He steps into the Father's will. His confidence and control comes out of his trust in his Father and his Father's will. He will not run from his Father's plan. It is his Father's will, and so he receives it.

As Jesus accepts the Father's will, Peter takes up arms to fight against it. He swings wildly and clips off part of Malchus' ear. This becomes the natural moment for the police and the officers to move in with their weapons, but before they can take a step, Jesus speaks and no one else moves. He picks up the ear and restores it in front of all the soldiers. Jesus says, "'No more of this!' And he touched the man's ear and healed him" (Lk 22:51). John describes this amazing scene masterfully, brilliantly, and succinctly. No one can miss the fact that

Jesus is the one that is in full control. "Put your sword away! Shall I not drink the cup the Father has given me?" he tells Peter (Jn 18:11).

I am glad to know that Jesus is always in that kind of control. I may be as confused as Peter was. I may be as ridiculous as Peter was. I may be as far from understanding what is taking place. I may be as perplexed and in as much inner chaos as Peter was. But that does not matter! Jesus is in control. Peter is a great example of how ridiculous it is for you and me to try to defend the Lord Jesus. The God of creation stands in the middle of the soldiers and temple leaders, and Peter takes up a single sword to try to protect him. One of the reasons Jesus did not call for twelve legions of angels is because he could have taken care of the situation very well without a single angel. He did not need angels to help him.

What a beautiful picture of how preposterous our fleshly activities are when they are not controlled by the Spirit, not led by the Spirit, and not within the will of God. We see the King appearing to suffer, and we rise to his defense, but many times, when we rise to his defense, we are as ridiculous as Peter. God is in control. Three chapters later, after the resurrection, Jesus says to Peter, "When you are old you will stretch out your hands, and someone else will dress you and lead you where you do not want to go" (Jn 21:18). Exactly what happens to Jesus in the garden arrest will happen to Peter as he follows Christ. His hands will be bound, and he will go to a death he does not want. According to tradition, when that day came, Peter requested to be crucified upside down, because he did not feel worthy to be crucified the way his master was crucified. The way of the Master became the way of his disciple, and Peter did not shrink back from the suffering involved in the Father's will for him. When the day came for Peter to really be put to the test, he did not lash out in confusion and uncertainty; he was not ridiculous or afraid. He took the will of God the way his Master had done. This should give all of us hope who have ever tried to defend Jesus in our own strength and proved ourselves silly and out of sync with the Spirit. If God can take Peter from ridiculous to triumphant, he can do the same for you and for me.

This story also illustrates beautifully Jesus' concern for his eleven disciples. Jesus is being arrested; he is the one being taken to trial. He is the one who, in the matter of a few hours, will be stretched out on a cross, but he is not thinking of himself. In his moment of surrender, he steps out to protect his friends. Why does he do this? Why does he not request his disciples to stand with him? John writes, "This happened so that the words he had spoken would be fulfilled: 'I have not lost one of those you gave to me'" (Jn 18:9).

Jesus' primary concern at this moment is the protection of Peter and his friends. How concerned is he? I think that is the main reason for the story of Malchus being given as it is. The soldiers have every right to arrest Peter and carry him away with Jesus for resisting arrest and attacking a temple guard. Jesus reaches out and restores that ear. He defends and protects Peter. There will be days when Jesus will have to perform a miracle to protect you, but he is able—and he is not only able; he is willing. He is not only willing; his work depends on ridiculous people like you and me. He is far more concerned about us than anything else, and so he moves to protect his own.

This story shines a light on the magnificence of what God came to do at Pentecost. Peter spends three years with Jesus, believes in Jesus, follows Jesus, loves Jesus, even raises a sword to fight for Jesus. Still, Peter's heart is full of uncertainty and fear. At Pentecost, when the Holy Spirit comes and cleanses his heart and fills him with the Spirit of Christ himself, Peter is no longer ridiculous. He is a chosen instrument of God and chooses to do the will of his Father. I love the fullness of the story. We identify with Peter in our own carnal fleshly ways, and we can see Peter's transformation as he is filled with the fullness of the Holy Spirit. The Spirit enables Peter—and will enable us—to live no longer in the flesh but in the power of the Spirit and in the ways of the Master.

One final point to this story intrigues me: what a compelling and continuous witness Jesus leaves in Jerusalem! Not too many hours after this scene in the garden, Jesus is dead and buried in a tomb. Then not too many hours later he is resurrected. As far as we know, he never walks this garden pathway again, and he never travels the streets of Jerusalem again. Caiaphas, the high priest, is the one who orchestrates this arrest. He sends the officers to the temple, he appeals to the Roman guard to go along, and he contracts with Judas for the death of Jesus. What do you think happened when Malchus went into Caiaphas's office to report on the arrest? I imagine it went something like this:

"Well, Malchus," Caiaphas demands roughly, "did you get him?"

Malchus hesitates, and then responds quietly as he rubs his right ear, "Yes sir, we got him."

"Did you have any trouble? What about from that big, loud fisherman? Did he cause trouble?"

"Well, yes, sir. He caused a little trouble," replies Malchus, rubbing his ear again, making sure it is still there.

"What was the trouble? Out with it! I want to know what happened."

"Sir, that big fisherman—Peter, they call him—well sir, he sliced off my ear."

Caiaphas stares at Malchus' ear. "Your ear looks okay to me."

"Sir, that is the problem." says Malchus, "Are you sure we want to arrest *him*?"

I suppose on Monday morning after the crucifixion, Caiaphas, who has been hearing rumors all night long, looks at his servant, and all he can see is Malchus' right ear. Could the man who heals ears conquer death? That question must have flashed through his mind. Malchus' ear is God's last love note to Caiaphas, God's last attempt to save that old high priest through his mercy and grace. From that moment, every time he looked at Malchus, he saw Jesus' testimony: that when the soldiers came to arrest him and to kill him, Jesus could only do them good. I believe that, pretty soon, Caiaphas transferred Malchus to another position so he no longer had to stare at God's love note to him.

Do you suppose Malchus became a believer? All I know is that the rest of his days Malchus bore in his body evidences of Jesus' grace.

Every day, we bear a similar witness somewhere. I wonder about the Roman soldiers. I suppose when they got time to sit down and talk, they said, "Do you suppose we arrested the wrong fellow? Maybe we ought to have gone and arrested Caiaphas instead. How could he have healed Malchus while we were arresting him?" You can look at the bitterest enemies of Jesus, and, if you know enough, you will find somewhere in their lives a testimony to the grace and the love of Christ. He never leaves himself without a love note, without a witness, and he leaves it in the most remarkable places. Did you know that one of Genghis Khan's wives was a Christian? He sticks his people in the places where the witness needs to be made.

I was doing graduate work at Brandeis University many years ago; Brandeis is a Jewish University. There were not too many Christians there and fewer Protestants. I was sitting in an upstairs, interior room in the library. One wall was covered with glass and you could look down on the student fellowship room. I was sitting over against the other wall so there would be no distraction, and I was buried in some ancient literature. Slowly, I began to be aware of a noise, something unusual. Then I became conscious I was hearing the strains of Handel's *Hallelujah Chorus* in the midst of this Jewish University. I got up and walked over to the glass wall and looked down. The fellowship room was full of young Jews and Jewesses, listening to the greatest witness to Jesus ever written in music. Their bodies were moving, keeping time to music, "He shall reign forever and ever. King of Kings and Lord of Lords." I was astonished by the love of the Father that will ensure the witness to his Son goes into every part of society and life.

If we miss Christ, it will not be because we have turned down one witness to him. It will be a million signals that we have missed. Our total life is immersed in him, but we are too busy to see. We do not want to take the time or pay the price. We have to listen if we want to hear him, and we have to look if we want to see him. Some of us get so close and miss him, because we do not pay attention to his love notes. As Paul said, we will be without excuse in that day, because his divine power and Godhead have been revealed in the creation in a million ways.

Now, one last thing: this was the last time, as far as we know, that Jesus and Judas ever met. I challenge you to sit down and read these four accounts and see what Jesus had to say to this disciple. He really had nothing to say to Judas at this point; he does not beg or plead for his former disciple's soul. He simply lets him do what he has come to do. Do you know there can come a time in a person's life when Christ has nothing more to say? When a person reaches that point where he knows the truth and consciously, deliberately, maliciously, chooses against it, there will be a silence that comes at the other end. God has nothing more to say.

On at least three occasions in the life of Jesus, he has nothing more to say. He has nothing more to say to Judas; he has chosen his path, and Jesus accepts his choice. The rich young ruler is another example. The young man walks away sorrowfully, and the text tells us that Jesus loved him, but he did not call him back. The man has made his choice, and Christ has nothing more to say to him. Herod is the third example. Herod seems somewhat pleased when he realizes he is going to get a chance to see Jesus. His carnal, malicious old soul has wearied of his own magicians, and the crowd says that Jesus can do remarkable things. I think Herod anticipates seeing a miracle. When they bring Jesus in, Jesus never even looks at Herod. When Herod speaks to him, Jesus never acknowledges that Herod is a king. I suppose he is the only person that Jesus ever snubs, but what is there to say to a man who cut off the head of John the Baptist? John had preached to Herod. Herod had had long sessions with John, and, if he would not listen to John, Jesus has nothing more to say to him. If we do not live in the light we have, Jesus will let us walk into the darkness.

There is a time when a person makes a choice, and God has nothing more to say. When he goes away, he walks away from the One who is goodness and light, and God has little to offer one hardened in his impenitence. He just lets him walk away. I trust that there are none of us to whom God has no more to say. I hope that, at least, all of us are in the category of a ridiculous Peter, because that is where the hope of the world lies. It lies in those whom Jesus moves to protect and to care for because they are his own, because they are the ones that he can make the light of the world and the salt to our generation.

Come to the One who called you and chose you to be his own. He cares for you. Let him do that work in your heart so he can move you from living in the flesh to living in the Spirit and make even you and me adequate witnesses to Jesus Christ, the Master and sovereign Lord of all.

2

The Unexpected Savior

THE GOSPEL OF JOHN

Papa loved the book of John. It was his favorite Gospel because of John's theological emphasis all the way through his writings. This sermon, however, did not come out of the theological discourses in John but out of four stories John told that illustrated his theology in a beautiful way: Christ comes knocking, he comes on a donkey, he comes washing feet, and he dies on a cross. Christ comes neither the way we want him nor the way we expect him, but he does come, and he gives us the opportunity to receive him.

Papa had received Jesus Christ as a thirteen-year-old boy in a very powerful way at Indian Springs Holiness Camp Meeting, and that encounter became the foundation stone of his life. His life was lived in openness to that One who had come to him as a teenager. Even in a life of Christian ministry, Christianity never became formal or functional for him; it was never a set of rules or tradition. Christ makes himself available to every person who will open their hearts to him, and Papa lived in openness to Christ.

Education added to, never detracted from, his sense of the personal proximity of Christ. He would say that studying gave him more questions than answers, but the questions became promises of God's answers. Christianity, for him, was neither a personal identity nor a career path; it was a living encounter with the Christ of history.

He wanted to live in that reality every moment of every day, and he wanted his actions to be consistent with his own experience of Christ. As he grew older and his body became more frail, he worked to keep the sense of the personal nearness of Christ. Prayer and worship became ways of life for him, and Christ became in even deeper ways the refuge of his soul.

This sermon epitomizes the sacrifice of Christ on our behalf. He left all the glory to become available to us—as one who knocks, one who rides a donkey, one who kneels, and one who is crucified. When we accept him as such, he becomes Lord in our lives and we join him not in power plays for the salvation of the world but in willing and loving self-sacrifice. Christ does not force himself on us, and he does not impose himself. He does not come where he is not welcome. Papa knew that welcoming Christ into one's life, home, and family was the happiest and the most fulfilling thing that one could do. He testified to the fact that Christ was better than all his gifts, and, when he comes into a human life, that life and all those around it feel the goodness, the light, and the joy of his presence.

He came to that which was his own, but his own did not receive him. (John 1:11)

"Blessed is he who comes in the name of the Lord! Blessed is the king of Israel!" Jesus found a young donkey and sat on it, as it is written: "Do not be afraid, Daughter of Zion; see, your king is coming, seated on a donkey's colt." (John 12:13–15)

Jesus knew that the Father had put all things under his power, and that he had come from God and was returning to God; so he got up from the meal, took off his outer clothing, and wrapped a towel around his waist . . . and began to wash his disciples' feet." (John 13:3–5)

Carrying his own cross, he went out to the place of the Skull . . . . There they crucified him, and with him two others—one on each side and Jesus in the middle." (John 19:17–18)

Palm Sunday gives us a picture of Jesus as the King of Israel when all of Jerusalem turns out to see the Messiah, and the children lead the crowd in singing praises, shouting, "Hosanna! Blessed is he who comes in the name of the Lord!" (Jn 12:13). Israel has been waiting for nineteen hundred years for their king, David's greater son, to come. The triumphal entry of Jesus indicates that their king finally has come, and they celebrate him. In that crowd, some Greeks come and find Philip, one of Jesus' disciples, and they say to Philip, "Sir, we would like to see Jesus" (Jn 12:21). Philip goes and finds his brother Andrew, and together they tell Jesus. One of the most significant passages in all of the New Testament is Jesus' response. Jesus is now within a few days of the crucifixion, and he knows that he is heading for the cross. The whole city has been lauding him, praising him, and now the disciples inform him that the gentiles in this Jewish city want to see him. All of a sudden, in the midst of Jesus' very Jewish triumphal entry, a reminder is given of that bigger world for which Christ came to give his life. When Philip and Andrew come and tell Jesus of the Greeks' request to see him, Jesus is immediately reminded of his mission for the larger world. He has come not just for the those who knew God, not just for the righteous, not just for the good, but for the whole world. These gentile Greeks represent that larger world. He knows that the only way that the larger world can ever be saved is the way of the cross. God has given his only begotten Son, knowing the cross awaits him. He says, "As Moses lifted up the snake in the wilderness, so the Son of Man must be lifted up," speaking of the crucifixion (Jn 3:14). Jesus knows the gentiles are there. They represent the whole world, and he says, "There's no way that world can be reached except by the way of the cross on Friday." Jesus responds to the need of the larger world with this surprising expression, "The hour has come for the Son of Man to be glorified" (Jn 12:23).

A throne, not a cross, is what the Jewish followers of Jesus anticipate by this statement, especially in light of the triumphal entry. Just a few days before he faces the cross, Jesus says, "The hour has come for the Son of Man to be glorified" (Jn 12:23). How is he going to be glorified? He is going to be glorified by crucifixion, suffering, dying, burial, and resurrection. Jesus explains his statement in the next verse: "Very truly I tell you, unless a kernel of wheat falls to the ground and dies, it remains only a single seed. But if it dies, it produces many seeds. Anyone who loves their life will lose it, while anyone who hates their life in this world will keep it for eternal life" (Jn 12:24–25). Jesus first calls his disciples by saying, "Follow me." We are never first. We will never get ahead of him. He does not say "Obey me!" but "Follow me!" He goes first and then invites us to follow him. He invites us to follow him to the cross. I have always been glad for the scene in the Garden of Gethsemane when Jesus admits to God that he does not want to be crucified, because it indicates that Jesus is as human as we are. He does not enjoy the prospect of suffering, shame, rejection, or physical death, but he willingly goes where his Father asks him to go, knowing his Father's name will be glorified.

I suspect there is no profounder principle of Christian life asserted anywhere in Scripture than in this passage where Jesus speaks of a kernel of wheat falling into the ground and dying, losing its identity in a new creation. The kernel dies alone, but, if it loses its life, it gains new life and produces much fruit. This concept was the most difficult one for the Jewish people of Jesus' day to grasp, and I am convinced it is the most difficult thing for the Church today to understand and accept.

Jesus, by his word and his life, illustrates the universal principle that no self-centered life can be fruitful. No life is fruitful until the person loses an interest in gaining his own way and surrenders himself to something bigger and nobler than himself—to God. When human persons lose their lives, they really begin to live. This thinking is unnatural to everything within us because we want to protect our interests. We want to take care of our concerns and our well-being, our security, and our pleasures. Jesus declares that as we give our rights to ourselves to the One who created and redeemed us he gives us life in himself and makes us a blessing to others.

Jesus proves that this is the way persons find life—even the divine persons. Not even God can be fruitful without self-sacrifice. I have always thought that God can speak and do what he pleases. If he wants to save the world, he can do it in a word—he certainly has enough power. But power never saves anybody; God could not save the world without giving himself, and that is what we believe happens in Christ Jesus, that "God was reconciling the world to himself in Christ" (2 Cor 5:19). If God cannot be fruitful without sacrificing himself, how can we be fruitful if we hold on to our lives and control them?

When Jesus comes, living out this self-giving love, the Jews do not know what to do with him. Israel rejects Christ for the very reasons that they ought to accept him. Jewish people had their ideas about what the Christ was going to be like. They believed that he would have sovereign power. The context for the Messiah would be a throne, a crown, a scepter, servants, and a kingdom. Then God comes in Christ in the most unlikely and humble way one could imagine. I have a lot of sympathy for the innkeeper in Bethlehem. How is he to know that he is displacing God? Who could ever believe that God would come in a peasant girl's body? Israel expects God to come in power and glory, and he comes in the same messy way that you and I come: through physical birth.

The life of Jesus is filled with the unexpected. Jesus turns up in places and in ways and with people that one would never expect from the Messiah. Think of the Samaritan woman, Zacchaeus, and the woman who anointed him with perfume. This is always the way he comes. His unexpected ways surprise and shake people, and many will not receive him because he does not come the way they want him to, the way they expect him.

The Gospel of John gives four examples of Jesus' unexpected way of salvation. Four pictures of Christ coming in John illustrate that Jesus comes exactly the reverse of how the Jews expected him to come. John gives the first picture in John 1:11: "He came to that which was his own, but his own did not receive him." God comes to that which belongs to him, his very creation, and his own creation does not receive its creator. The first picture in the Gospel of John is a God who can be rejected. Christ does not impose himself on his creation; he does not come in such a way that people do not have a choice to receive him. He does not impinge on human freedom, but he comes "rejectable." The Jews of the first century had the option to receive Christ or to resist him, and we have the same freedom to open ourselves to receive him or to close the door of our hearts to him.

John revisits this theme in Revelation 3:20, "Here I am! I stand at the door and knock. If anyone hears my voice and opens the door, I will come in and eat with that person, and they with me." Out of all the paintings of Christ that I have ever seen, the one that has impressed me most is Holman Hunt's painting of this tender verse in Revelation, "The Light of the World." Hunt painted two versions of it: the first is at Oxford and the second, larger one is in St. Paul's Cathedral in London. I have been to London twice, and each time I have gone to St. Paul's to see this Holman Hunt painting. The painting is life-sized, and in it Christ has on royal robes; he is our king. He has on priestly robes as well; he is our high priest. He has a crown on his head, and there is a kingly stature about his whole figure. He has a lantern in his hand that casts its light about his feet. He is standing at a doorway, but there is no handle on the door. The greenery has grown up over the door, so you know that the door has not been opened for a long time. He stands knocking.

I looked at that painting and enjoyed the beauty of it. It is very impressive. The irony of the scene never came home to me until the last three or four years. The one thing a king never does is knock at anybody's door. Kings have a whole retinue of people that go before them to open all the doors. Watch the president of the United States come into a press conference, and you will notice that he never knocks on any door. Knocking implies the possibility of rejection. Power and position and pomp do not expose themselves to rejection. Kings do not leave themselves open to rejection. No human experience is more painful or humiliating that being rejected. I would rather suffer physical pain than have the people I care about reject me, and I suspect you feel the same way.

The eternal God puts himself in a rejectable, vulnerable position. I first looked at that painting of Jesus in St. Paul's in 1955. The second time I saw it was in 1974. Do you know what interested me most the second time I saw it? He was still knocking. He had been there nineteen years, knocking. How far will God go to reach you and me? He is willing to stand knocking until the last one has had a chance to open the door.

There's not another god anywhere in the world like Jesus. The other gods have people beating down their pathways to get to them. Our God comes to get us! And when he draws near to his people, he gives us the privilege of receiving or rejecting him. He appears in vulnerability, in willing self-exposure.

The second picture of Jesus coming in John is even more unexpected; it occurs on Palm Sunday. This celebration is the culmination of three years of ministry, filled with miracles and teaching. He is the wisest of men that had ever come. The people have seen lepers cleansed, the blind given sight, and lame people walking. Just a few days before this final trip outside the city of Jerusalem, in Bethany, he raises Lazarus, who has been dead four days. It is the final demonstration of his power, and the whole city knows about it, including the temple authorities. The Jewish leaders believe the whole world is going after Jesus, and they are scrambling to figure out how to stop his influence. It is Passover week, and so they come out to the edge of the city to see if he will come into Jerusalem. When he comes, the crowds begin to strip the branches from the palm trees and to take the clothes off their backs to lay them in the roadway in front of him. The people are chanting, "Hosanna to the Son of David, Hosanna to the King of Israel" (see Jn 12:13). Jesus sees the crowds and he looks around for an appropriate way to enter the city. He chooses a donkey and its foal to be the means of taking him into the city.

I read that passage for years before I realized that this event is the fulfillment of an Old Testament prophecy in Zechariah 9:9, "Rejoice greatly, Daughter Zion! Shout, Daughter Jerusalem! See, your king comes to you, righteous and victorious, lowly and riding on a donkey, on a colt, the foal of a donkey." Jesus does exactly what the prophet said the Messiah would do. He comes into the city, riding on a donkey and acknowledging openly that he is the one for whom Israel had waited and hoped. He fulfills the role of the Messiah. The next verse in Zechariah says, "I will take away the chariots from Ephraim and the warhorses from Jerusalem." Could it be that he chose a donkey in deliberate contrast to a horse? When a Roman general rode through the city of Jerusalem, he rode a well-trained military horse. When a Babylonian emperor came through, he rode a royal horse. When an Egyptian Pharaoh came, he came in a chariot pulled by a team of horses magnificently arrayed.

To ride a horse is a symbol of honor and power; to ride a donkey is a sign of humility and poverty. Lexington, Kentucky, is famous for its race horses, and a yearling that had never raced sold for over eight million dollars; the summer before, one sold for over ten million dollars. I asked a friend what the price for a donkey would be in Lexington, and he said that it would be less than one hundred dollars.

Solomon was known for his horse stables, but David hobbled the horses that his army captured, because his army was not supposed to put their trust in horses. The horse is the equivalent of the first military tank or the first military airplane—a military instrument that gives a significant advantage—but God wants his people to trust in him instead (Deut 17:16). The donkey is not the symbol of power or of pomp; it is the symbol of service and of humility. Jesus wants his people to know that his kingdom is much more of a donkey kingdom than a horse kingdom. Jesus says that, "the Son of Man did not come to be served, but to serve, and to give his life as a ransom for many" (Matt 20:28). The Jews reject this kind of a Messiah.

The third surprising picture of Jesus in John occurs later that week, on Thursday night of passion week in the Upper Room. Jesus gathers with his twelve disciples to celebrate the Passover. He takes a basin of water and a towel, kneels, and begins washing the feet of one of his disciples. Peter looks at him and says, "You shall never wash my feet" (Jn 13:8). I have sympathy for Peter. God wash my feet? Me wash his, maybe! I belong at his feet, but God does not belong at my feet. Peter wants Jesus to get up off his knees, and Jesus looks at him and declares, "If I do not wash you, you have no share with me" (Jn 13:8 ESV). Jesus washes their feet in the upper room with only his disciples present, because the city that couldn't understand him when he came on a donkey would never have understood why he knelt to wash their feet. No other religion in the world has anything like this self-giving God. How far will God go to reach you and me? He will get on his knees to wash our feet. He does downright ungodly things to get to the likes of you and me.

The final unexpected picture occurs on Friday of Holy Week. Outside the city on a hill, they nail Jesus to a cross. Anybody knows that when God comes, he should come wearing a crown, wielding a scepter, sitting on a throne. Jesus' crown is thorns; his scepter, a broken reed; and his throne, a cross. The Romans nail him to the cross, and the Jewish leaders look at the cross and declare it to be conclusive proof that Jesus is not the Son of God. For a man to die for his god is not news. Human history is full of that. When did anybody ever hear of a god dying for his creatures? If there were a god like that, that would be news. There *is* a God like this, and that news is the story of all stories: "For God so loved the world, that he gave his only begotten Son . . ." (Jn 3:16 KJV).

God, in Christ, is reconciling the world to himself on the cross. It is not just the priests who don't get it; the disciples do not know what to do with this God. They simply flee at the cross. They do not understand him; he does not fit any of their patterns or expectations. They know how God is supposed to come, and Jesus does not fit the role. They love him and believe him, but, at the cross, they just fade into the woodwork. Only the Roman centurion at the crucifixion recognizes him for who he truly is. The hardened soldier, the leader of the execution squad, has watched men die; in fact, he is the instrument of their deaths. While everyone else is standing below saying that Jesus cannot be the Christ, the Roman centurion looks up and hears him say, "Father, forgive them, for they do not know what they are doing" (Lk 23:24). That old executioner, a Roman gentile soldier, looks up and says, "Surely this man was the Son of God!" (Mk 15:39). That is the kind of person God is reaching for: one who can see what is right before him.

These four pictures amazed me; the uniqueness of the Christian God caused me to worship, and his willingness to win the hearts of his people caused my soul to rejoice in him. However, I was not done with surprises. I turned to the book of Revelation, and I found a greater shock than the four pictures in John. In the book of Revelation, there are four pictures of Christ, and they are the same pictures as in John's Gospel with one exception: all four pictures are reversed!

When Jesus comes the second time, he does not come knocking. Revelation 1:7 tell us he is coming in the clouds. He will come like lightning, and every eye will see him, and not a single door will be able to keep him out. Not a prison door, not a metal door, not a wooden door, not a door in our hearts. He will breach every door when he comes the second time.

When he comes the second time, he will not come on a donkey. Revelation 19 declares that he will come on a great white horse with a host behind him, with a two-edged sword coming out of his mouth like a flame of fire. And written across his thigh will be the title, "King of Kings and Lord of Lords!" (see Rev 19:11–16). He will come in power and glory.

When he comes the next time, he will not come washing people's feet. Revelation 6 explains that all the chief men of the earth—the kings, the emperors, the captains, the nobles—will be on their faces at his feet, pleading for the rocks and the mountains to fall on them and to hide them from the face of him that sits upon the throne and from the Lamb. The first time, we disposed of him. The second time, he will be the disposer of all things. When he comes again, he will not come on a cross; he will sit on a great white throne, and he will judge the nations of the earth and all men (Rev 19–20).

After reading the Revelation passages, I had my own revelation: when Jesus returns the second time, he will not come as Savior. Not a single act of salvation will be accomplished; not a single sin will be forgiven when Jesus appears the second time. Not a single broken relationship will be restored; not a single person will be released from sin by the demonstration of his power and his glory, his dominion and his authority, and his kingdom. Revelation 22:11 says, "Let the one who does wrong continue to do wrong; let the vile person continue to be vile; let the one who does right continue to do right; and let the holy person continue to be holy." When he comes in power and glory, it will be to fix everything the way it is.

It is only when self-sacrifice occurs that anything is ever saved. Not even God is exempt from that. If God wants to redeem, the only way he can redeem is by the sacrifice of himself. That is the reason the doctrine of the Trinity is essential to the Christian faith. There can be no atonement in Judaism because there is no triune godhead in whom sin can be atoned for by self-sacrifice. In Islam, there is no atonement; salvation can only be gained by works. Only a Person of the Trinity can take into himself our sins, with its consequences and its death. Only in the God of Scripture—the God who is Father, Son, and Holy Spirit— can atonement take place, and only where there is the sacrifice of oneself can there be anything redemptive. You know that is true if you stop to think. The thing that moves a person most deeply is not God's power, not his glory, not his crown and authority, but the sacrifice of himself at Calvary. That kind of love is hard to resist.

The only way the world is ever going to be saved is on the principle of Jesus' sacrifice, as followers of Jesus willingly enter into that sacrifice and give themselves for a lost world. He tells his disciples to follow him. As we enter into the fellowship of his sufferings, we create an opening for others to enter into that life as well. God desires that all believers join the fellowship of self-giving love that began in the heart of God. Jesus said, "As the Father has sent me, I am sending you" (Jn 20:21).

We want to save the world by having them come knock at our door. He said, "Go into all the world" (Mk 16:15; see also Matt 28:19). None of us will ever go as far as he went to reach us, to reach the world. We would like the world to come wash our feet. None of us will ever stoop as low as Jesus stooped for us. If you hit the absolute bottom, you will find he has been there before you. We want to save the world on the horse, with show and circumstance, not with lowliness and meekness. We want people coming to us instead of us going to them and suffering before them, kneeling to them, pleading with them. We want to do it from our protected place, not an unsafe place where they could destroy us.

Christy Wilson spent many years in Afghanistan and had a burden all his life for the Muslim world. He stated that Muslims sacrifice their lives to Allah so that Christians can die, but what if Christians would sacrifice their lives for Christ so that Muslims could live? If the Muslim world is ever going to be won, it will only be possible through self-giving love. If anybody's ever won, that is the way they are won. It is a universal eternal law that if I keep my life, it will be fruitless. That is the reason Christ asks for the whole heart. We want to give him part, to protect a little bit so that we have a little room for self-interest, a little security. If I turn the whole thing loose to him, what will he do with it? Surrender can be downright terrifying!

When I gave God full control of my life, he said to me, "Dennis, you still have your thumb on your life." I found that I could not let go of my grasp, so I just looked up to him and said, "Lord, crack these knuckles of mine. Crack them so hard that I can't hold on to my life anymore. Somehow or other break my hold on me, so you can get all of me and do with me what you please with me." I found that he was willing to come and set me free from myself. All our lives are sterile and dead until they are delivered from self-control and self-dominion.

After he has delivered us from self-interest, he looks at us and says, "Follow me!" Remember, Philip said, "Lord, show us the Father and that will be enough for us" (Jn 14:8). Jesus said, "Don't you know me Philip, even after I have been among you such a long time? Anyone who has seen me has seen the Father. . . . Don't you believe that I am in the Father, and the Father is in me? . . ." (Jn 14:9–10). At the end of John, Jesus said, "Peace be with you! As the Father has sent me, I am sending you" (Jn 20:21). Jesus is the face of the Father, and he is sending the disciples out in his name. What is he sending us to do? He is sending us to do what Jesus did: to give our lives away for Jesus' sake. In the way the Father poured out the life of the Son for us, he is sending us so he can pour out our lives for God and for the world.

What if the Church really believed that? We have the resources to shape the world. We not only have the resources to shape the world, we have the resources to *win* the world. The reason it is not won is because we have neither understood nor wanted the way he is going to do it. I have been asking God to let me see this clearly enough that my life will be consumed by it, that my life will be a poured out as an offering unto him.

Oswald Chambers was sitting at the breakfast table with some friends one day. As they finished the breakfast somebody said, "Oswald, you pray."

He said, "Lord, help yourself to us today. Just help yourself to us today. You are welcome. Help yourself to all of us."[1]

Have you prayed that? If there is any corner of you that you haven't released to him, you ought not to let today pass without saying to him, "Lord, help yourself to all of me. Because what I keep is going to be dead and fruitless, but what you get is going to be fruitful and eternal."

---

1   The original reference to this story is unknown.

3

Our Way in Christ Jesus

JEREMIAH 10:23

Understanding personhood became, for Papa, one of the greatest intellectual quests of his life. His questions flowed out of an intense interest in the Trinity, a God of three persons who has created human persons in his own image. Papa wanted desperately to know what it meant to be a divine person and what it meant to be a human person. I started working with Papa when he was seventy-six and I was twenty-six; instantly, I was caught up in his study of personhood. He assigned me all kinds of reading to help him in his search to understand who we are and how we are made in God's image.

Jeremiah 10:23 was the verse that initially drew him into a biblical exploration of personhood: "I know, O LORD, that the way of man is not in himself, that it is not in man who walks to direct his steps" (ESV). It was in this one verse, in a rather obscure chapter, that Papa found an intellectual and theological key that unlocked the beginning of this mystery. The foundation of his understanding of personhood that came from this verse is that we are not complete in ourselves. Human persons are made for something beyond; we find our own identity as we relate in love to other persons, as we live in the webs of relationships in which God has placed us. Openness and reciprocity are the two keys that are essential for these relationships to work with other human persons. These webs of relationships mirror the divine relationship. The Father, Son, and Spirit live together in a relationship of love and self-giving that defines who they are in themselves and how they relate to the world. Papa wanted to talk personhood with everyone who came through our front door, so family members, teenagers, scholars, and anyone who would listen were caught up in this conversation about what it means to be a person.

His interest in the holiness message pushed him at this point. He believed we were made for God, made to be completed in him, to find ourselves in him. Holiness meant finding our lives as human persons in the conversation of the three divine persons. He believed that if we could say this right, every believer would want to enter into this intimacy with the triune God. This sermon was part of Papa's attempt to communicate the glory of God's design in creating human personhood.

As Papa neared the end of his life, his family was talking about the joy he would share with my grandmother when they were re-united in heaven. We were all thinking about the sweetness of that reunion when one family member said, "Well, we know for sure that he will be talking to her about personhood." We are confident that one of the joys of heaven for Papa will be continuing his study of personhood that began with Jeremiah 10:23.

I know, O Lord, that the way of man is not in himself, that it is not in man who walks to direct his steps. (Jeremiah 10:23 ESV)

Every human person faces two questions that determine the course of existence. The first question deals with the nature of God. Who is he and what is he like? The second most important question that a person ever faces is the question of who you and I are and what we are like. If we understand the nature of God and if we understand the nature of ourselves, there is a good chance that we will be able to live meaningful and effective lives in terms of service. When we have false views of God, then we are in trouble. In the same way, when we have a false understanding of ourselves, when we put false requirements upon ourselves or excuse ourselves from requirements that ought to be there, or do not understand what we are capable of and what should be expected of us, then we go wrong.

I want to deal with the question of what our nature is like, what human persons are. I am going to use Scripture and Christian theology, because the Scripture very clearly states that man is made in the image of God, and I am convinced that we never know who we are until we've faced God. When we have some conception of what he is, there is a chance then that we can know ourselves accurately and in a realistic way.

Wherever you turn in the history of theology, you will find that every major theologian has dealt somewhere with the question, "What is the nature of man?" Theologians, psychologists, and philosophers have all studied this all-important question. This is a crucial question, whether you are a social scientist, a political scientist, or a psychologist. What does it mean to be a human person? It is important not only for the scholars but also for the person in Christian ministry. What should you expect out of your people? What should you try to work to see achieved or accomplished in the lives of your people? What should you expect out of yourself before you go to them? Or, when you come to such things as marriage, what should you expect out of a marriage relationship? If we can understand what is a sound and a realistic view of the nature of man, that knowledge will be pertinent in the most intimate, the most practical, and the most personal relations that we have.

The text that I want to use is Jeremiah 10:23. I am going to use my own translation of this passage. The RSV is a very good translation; the King James, a satisfactory one; but I spent ten years studying Hebrew and five years teaching it, so I'm going to dare to just spell out for you what the Hebrew text says.

The English text that I have right here in front of me says, "I know, O LORD, that the way of man is not in himself, that it is not in man who walks to direct his steps" (ESV). The latter part of that text is quite adequate, but the first part does not reflect all that I think Jeremiah was speaking about. The verse starts, "I know, O Lord." Jeremiah uses the personal name for God in this verse, the name in the Old Testament, Yahweh, the name that we translate often in ritual and in hymnody as *Jehovah*; it is the personal name given to Israel for God, the name revealed to Moses at Mt. Sinai. The prophet is speaking to the God whom he knows by name, "I know, O Yahweh, that the way of man is not in himself, that it is not in man who walks to direct his steps."

In Hebrew, two different words are used for man. "I know O Yahweh, that *man's* way . . ."—the Hebrew word used is *adam*, the generic term for human beings, for homo sapiens, in the Old Testament. In Hebrew today, a "son of Adam"—a *ben adam*—is the Israeli word for a human being. It is a generic term that includes all of us, male and female. In Genesis 1:26–27, "God said, 'Let us make mankind [*adam*] in our image, in our likeness . . . so God created mankind in his own image, in the image of God he created them; male and female he created them." *Adam* is inclusive of the female as much as it is the male.

Jeremiah goes on to say to God, "I know, O Lord, about human persons, that their way is not in themselves." One begins to think of Old Testament passages where "way" is used. There's Psalm 1:6, "For the Lord watches over the way of the righteous, but the way of the wicked leads to destruction" and Proverbs 14:12, "There is a way that appears to be right, but in the end it leads to death." When Jesus came, he declared, "I am the way and the truth and the life. . . ." (Jn 14:6). In the Old Testament, a clear statement is made that *adam*'s way, the way of human persons, is not found within themselves.

Then you come to the second line of the verse, "I know, O Lord that *adam*'s way is not in himself; it is not in a man who walks to direct his steps." This second word for man is the Hebrew word *'ish*. This word is for a single individual, for the particular person rather than a word for human persons. The Hebrew of this verse covers the different aspects of personhood: the individual and the collective identity of human persons.

Something else that is significant here is in the expression, "who walks." Hebrew is a very cryptic language and expresses itself very briefly, so that just a few words sometimes express what English would take a paragraph to express. The phrase "who walks" is a Semitism for a goal-oriented creature, because human persons are created to walk, to move. They are created to walk somewhere, not idly or in circles. Human beings are driven by goals and dreams, and we are uncomfortable when we have wasted time. We may talk about loafing as great fun, but ultimately we all want to do meaningful work. Lack of focus and goals is actually destructive to personhood. You may be like me: I don't like to work, but I always like to *have* worked, and I'm always more comfortable when I have. Someone asked Paul Rees if he liked to write books, and he said, "No." He'd published between twenty-five and thirty books, and somebody said, "Well, why did you write all these books if you don't like to write?" He said, "I like to have written." I like that. We feel that we are supposed to accomplish something. There are few things that irritate us more than dead-end streets, especially if we have somewhere to be. We are created so that we like to get somewhere and accomplish something. Biblical theology describes this with a Greek word, *teleos*, which means that we are moving towards something in history.

This *telic* understanding of history was very different from Greek thought. In the ancient world, the Greeks had a cyclical view of time. Aristotle and Plato believed that if you wait long enough things will happen all over again. Time is not going forward, only around. Biblical thought is radically different than that: time has a beginning and an end. There is an eschatological element to our understanding of history. We are not going in circles; we are going somewhere. Not only is this true in our worldview, but it should be true in individual believers' lives. There should be something *telic* in our lives: we should have goals and objectives towards which we are striving and living.

We are goal-oriented creatures; we are supposed to get somewhere and supposed to do something, but the key as to how to do it and the directions as to how to get there are not in us. Humans are not self-contained units. We are not ends in ourselves; we are made for others. We do not draw our lives from ourselves; our way is not in us. That runs counter to most of modern thought—at least most of what modern thought espouses—because we want to emphasize our autonomy.

I turned on the radio the other day and got a part of one of these little excerpts, and the fellow was talking about the importance of having a good psychoanalyst, and he described how important it was to have a psychoanalyst that you're friendly with, because, he said, "What you want to do is get your life under control, under your own control." That's the supreme thing for modern man: to get life under control so we are not controlled by other people or other forces. That is considered freedom, maturity, and fulfillment, but this is not the biblical paradigm for finding God's way for one's life or for finding one's personal identity.

We had on our staff at Asbury College a fellow who was our chief business officer, and he loved to fly prop planes. He was a big, tall, six-foot-five guy, and I always wondered how he even fit into the tiny planes he liked to fly. One day, he took me flying with him and as we were talking about flying he said to me, "Dennis, there're two things in every plane; it doesn't matter how big it is or how small. In every plane, you have to have a compass and a horizon."

I understood what the compass was: it told us the difference between east and west and north and south, but I had no idea about a horizon. He explained it to me, "The horizon tells you how the plane sits in the air in relation to the surface of the earth. In other words, it tells you which way is up and which is down."

I was surprised and said, "Come on, Harry, don't tell me you're so stupid that you can't tell the difference between up and down."

Without offense, he looked back at me and assured me that he was not the stupid one. He said, "When you get into the clouds where you can't see the surface of the earth, if you're moving fast enough, you cannot tell which way is up and which way is down." A pilot, like all human beings, does not have an internal frame of reference. He must have one from outside himself.

I was talking to a fellow who flew jets for United Airlines for a while but, before that, he flew in the Air Force in the Korean war and was a jet fighter. His wing tip buddy crashed his jet into the ground at full speed into the side of a freight train, because he thought the red lights on the caboose of the freight train were the wing tip lights of the jet next to him. He had no notion of where he was in relation to the surface of the earth.

We must have a frame of reference for direction, and I am convinced we have to have something extrinsic to ourselves for mental health. If you want a person to come apart and go to pieces, you isolate that person. Daniel Defoe wrote about that in his story of Robinson Crusoe. Do you remember the incredible delight and also total panic when Crusoe found the footstep in the sand? He'd have given anything in the world for human companionship, but he was scared to death it might not be friendly fellowship, so he was torn. I question whether anybody can keep his balance who does not have a context of safety in which he can relate to others.

I had a chance to visit an old castle in Scotland, and in it they had a dungeon where they had put many religious leaders. This castle was well known for its dungeon because it had what was called a bottle dungeon. The bottle dungeon was cut down into pure granite. There was a shaft about thirty inches across, and that shaft was cut down through solid stone for about six feet and then it was cut out larger, but instead of being cut out square like a room or rectangular like a room, it was cut out circularly. It was cut out like a top (or a bottle). There was no corner anywhere in it. There was no way to escape, and nobody ever did. Once a day, they came and lifted the lid off. A little light came in, and they dropped the guy's food down and he had to catch what he could. What he didn't catch this way, he had to pick up off the floor, and I don't think they were cleaning up corpses and refuse in between occupants. Everyone who was dropped in that dungeon quickly went insane. When they were pulled out, they were completely disoriented as to the nature of reality, except for one man. When they pulled this one man back up, he was in his right mind, so his captors asked him about it. He said, "I had six pebbles in my pocket, and I'd take those six pebbles and move them from one pocket to another, and there were always six, and they never changed." There was one unchanging reality in his life; all the rest was total subjectivity. He had an external frame of reference that enabled him to keep his sanity.

If people get to the place where they have no external frame of reference, they begin to hallucinate, their imagination runs wild, and there is no way, ultimately, that they can tell the difference between reality and unreality. I think that's some of what Jeremiah was saying when he said, "I know, O LORD, that man's way (*adam*'s way) is not in himself. It is not in an individual, who was made to walk, to direct his steps." We do not operate correctly unless we have an external frame of reference.

There are many other scriptures that fit with this Jeremiah passage, but just let me mention one. In John 9, Jesus says, "As long as it is day, we must do the works of him who sent me. Night is coming, when no one can work. While I am in the world, I am the light of the world" (Jn 9:4–5). Think for a minute about that simple statement about working while one has the light, because when the night comes no man can work. There is no lighting system in you and me. If we want to get anywhere, we can only do it when a light extrinsic to ourselves shines upon our pathway. Otherwise, we'll be left in our own darkness, in our wandering, and in our blindness. I dare you to read through the Gospel of John and notice the passages where Jesus speaks of himself. Chapters 1, 3, 8, 9, and 12 all elaborate on this idea of Jesus as the light of the world.

The conception and birth of Jesus are not the beginning of his life. He lived somewhere else before he came to Bethlehem and, when he ascended into Heaven, he went somewhere else. Historically we say that he stands at the right hand of the Father, interceding for us, and he was incarnated as our Savior. Our salvation is from beyond. It came from beyond in Jesus Christ and went to the beyond in the ascension, and if I am to know salvation I must be related to a world that is beyond mine—one I cannot see, touch, feel, or measure.

Our world doesn't want to put its faith in a world it can't see. One of the reasons is because we don't want to be dependent and we want to be autonomous; we want to stand on our own two feet. I think that's the reason that you get the emphasis in our day on self-realization, self-actualization, and self-fulfillment.

I came across a little book by Paul Vitz of New York University; he was a psychology professor and taught for years on self-actualization and self-realization. As he taught, it slowly began to dawn on him that what he was teaching did not fit with reality. His job was to teach what he no longer believed to be true. Eventually, he came to an intellectual crisis in his life: would he teach what he did not believe matched reality? Ultimately, he wrote a book called *Psychology as Religion*. In this book, he does not rule out the value of psychology, but he rules out psychology when it becomes a religion. Many people believe in the old Socratic notion that if they look deeply enough and long enough inside the self, they will find the answer to life's problems within themselves. Vitz found that this did not fit with life; people are made for something beyond themselves.

I have become convinced that this was the heart of Eve's decision in the creation story. The serpent's temptation was that if Eve ate, she would become as a god. A god was a self-contained entity, independent and without restraint supposedly. The serpent challenged her to live her own life out of her own resources and in her own way. Somehow, it still comes as a shock to us to believe that lie isn't true.

I had a friend who was one of the brightest people I have ever known. He knew more unnecessary information than any man I had ever met. He was on the faculty of a major university, and he was widely published in the field of neurological psychology. He had a son who was a Boy Scout, and the son wanted to go on a Scout trip into the Canadian woods, so my friend signed up to go with his son. He wanted to be a good father and thought this was a good way to spend time with his son. He liked his son's scoutmaster. He was a young guy, optimistic, friendly, cordial—just a good guy. My friend told me his surprise at the end of the first day, when the scoutmaster pulled out a little book and began reading. He was reading the New Testament and after he finished he said, "Let's pray." My friend was shocked. He said to me later as he was recounting this story, "You know, the ridiculous thing was that, when he prayed, he sounded as though he thought somebody was listening."

My friend was perplexed. The scoutmaster seemed rational all day long, but the next evening he pulled out his little book and read a passage. Then he bowed his head and spoke to One who was unseen. My friend watched him and began to think to himself, "That guy's a very wholesome guy. He's exactly like what I wish I could get my patients to become: optimistic, friendly, happy, hopeful, charitable, concerned about other people. He is just wholesome." Finally, one night a horrible thought came to him. He thought to himself, "The scoutmaster is not only the kind of guy I wish my patients were like. I would like to be like him." He was a doctor of the human psyche, and he could not produce people like that scoutmaster. "I had another horrible thought," he said, "Do you suppose what he does each night, reading and praying, has something to do with his wholesomeness, his happiness, his contentment, his faith, and all the rest?"

One day my friend decided to try to imitate the scoutmaster. He told me that an interesting change began to take place in him. He got back to his university and thought with grief of his patients. He wanted them to find the inner joy he was beginning to find. He knew he couldn't tell them. That would be inconsistent with his discipline, but he thought he could pray for them in secret and not tell them. He decided to try it.

One day one of his partners on the faculty came to him and said, "What new techniques are you trying these days?'"

"None, standard stuff. Why?"

"You're doing something different. We can all tell."

He said, "What do you mean I'm doing something different?"

"Well," he said, "We've been talking about you; you're having a much higher success rate than you previously had. What are you doing different?"

This was the beginning of his Christian witness. In describing the change to me he said, "Dennis, the battle of my life was to believe there was a world out there I couldn't see, a world out there I couldn't touch, a world out there I couldn't measure, that I couldn't control. You see, I'd been indoctrinated in a learning system that had taught me that I should be in control of my world. The resurrection of Christ shook me all to pieces because it taught me to believe in a world that I could not control. The surrender of my life was at the point of believing in the personal resurrection of Christ. When I came to that point, life began to be different."

My friend began to draw from resources outside himself and his own life. He had lived his life up to that time on his own, and then he came to the place where he found resources that were not his own, and then he wanted to share those resources. Once one receives, one wants to share, but so often we fight God's gift. We don't like to receive because that makes us dependent. We don't want to be dependent; we want to stand on our own feet and not owe anyone anything.

When I was a pastor, one of the hardest things I ever had to do in a rural country parish down in the cabbage patches and swamps of North Carolina was to accept gifts. I had to learn, and it didn't come naturally. You can see the sinfulness of the human psyche more at this point than anywhere else: when we do not want to receive God's goodness.

I have become convinced that there are four nots that need to be faced in terms of who we are as human persons. If we misunderstand this, we will never see beyond ourselves to the other. The first is that we are *not self-originating*. Not a single person chose to be given life, not to say anything about producing one's own life. Every person's life, except for the first person of the blessed Trinity, is something received. The minute I bump into any person I have never seen before, I know he had a mother and a father. Life is given; it's not self-originating. We try to cover that up, but all life is a gift. Gratitude is an appropriate attitude for a person who understands the true nature of the human creature.

We also are *not self-sustaining*. We draw our life from outside ourselves. How long can a person live without food? Moses and Jesus fasted for forty days, but no one is going to live much longer than that if they do not have life-sustaining nourishment. Most of us, three times a day, celebrate our dependence by eating. How long can you live without water? A person can only survive a few days without water. We must have something outside of ourselves for survival. What is even more necessary than food and water? Breath. How long can you live without oxygen, without breathing? They say that after two minutes of not breathing death begins to take place in the cells of your brain. Approximately eighteen times every minute, you pay tribute to the fact that you are not self-sustaining. A person has to be pretty blind to believe he or she is autonomous. Life is a gift that is maintained from outside of our own bodies. Three times a day and eighteen times a minute we celebrate a theological truth: a person's way is not in himself.

One of the most magnificent discourses in the life of Jesus is after he fed the five thousand men—and who knows how many women and children—with those five loaves and two fish. The next day the Jews came to see him. They wanted to keep him around as king. And he said to them that they should not be concerned with the physical bread, but with the Bread that comes from heaven. What is he saying? Human persons are made by every word that proceeds out of the mouth of God; our lives are not in ourselves but in him. He said, "I am the bread of life" (Jn 6:35). Human life is not in human individuals; we are not created to be self-sustaining but receiving. We don't just need to receive physical things like food and air; our sustenance is in Christ. Communion is the symbol that we receive our salvation and our life from outside ourselves.

Human persons are *not self-fulfilling*. I heard Chuck Colson tell about visiting death row on Easter Sunday morning in Indianapolis.[1] He said, "I always try to visit death row when I'm in a prison. It's the most dehumanizing experience that can come to a man, isolation from other human beings; it's hellish."

"We walked down the corridor of death row, and every single man was asleep at eight o'clock. What else was there to do? But down at the end in the last cell the light was on. As we got close to it, we called, 'Bill!' and a man responded."

Two years before they had been there, and this fellow had found Christ. Colson said, "We had an Easter service at eight o'clock in the morning on death row. All around us were hollow eyes and dehumanized men, and then I looked at Bill, and his eyes were alert and his face was smiling. I looked at him and said, 'Bill, I'm sorry we couldn't let you know we were coming. The warden wouldn't tell us whether we could come until this morning, so we just found out a few minutes ago that we could come.'"

The prisoner looked back at him, and said, "Chuck, that's alright. I knew you'd come back. You'd been here before, you'd talked with me about Christ, you led me to Christ, and I knew you'd come back."

Chuck asked him, "How do you survive?"

"Oh," he responded, "They may have my body in here, but that is all they've got."

Now what was that prisoner doing? He was drawing his life from a context that those who were around him could not see. They did not know and it did not even exist as far as they were concerned. But there he was, witnessing that "the way of man is not in himself." Our fulfillment is not in us.

Fourth, we are *not self-explanatory*. There is no way that you can take a human being and explain what a human being is from one other human being. There is no such thing as a typical human being. There must be two to bring one into life. If you get me and do not get my wife, Elsie, you have only gotten half. That is the reason God says, "Let us

---

1 The date and location of Colson's sermon are unknown.

make [*adam*] in our own image, in our likeness . . . . So God created mankind in his own image, in the image of God he created them; male and female he created them" (Gen 1:26–27). From the very beginning, we have never been self-explanatory. This is one of my problems with homosexuality; there is no life in it. Our diversity makes a way for life and for creativity.

Human beings are most fulfilled when they are doing something for someone else. In a pastorate, one of the things that always excited me was when I developed a pastoral relationship with a young couple and they had their first child. I loved visiting the mother in the hospital. Oftentimes I would arrive within a few hours of the child being born. I would visit the father and the mother with the baby lying there next to her, and I would see the utter fulfillment on her face. Her fulfillment came in another.

In contrast, God is *self-originating*. I am sure you have heard that old question your kid asked, "Daddy, who made God?" And you said, "Nobody made God. He's the only one who's self-originating, self-sustaining." Jesus said that his Father had life in himself, and he gave to the Son life in himself. Jesus could say, "I am . . . the life. . . ." (Jn 14:6). You and I receive life; Jesus *is* life. Nothing in Scripture indicates that God had to create to be fulfilled. There was a joy and a fulfillment before the creation. It may have been augmented after the creation, but there is nothing in Scripture or in classical theology to reflect that God needed anything more for fulfillment.

I read through the Koran at one time. I had studied three years in a Jewish university, so I knew a bit about Judaism, but not about Islam. I had studied Arabic, so I decided to read the Koran. One thing that you will never find in the Koran is the statement, "God is love." There are passages where it says, "Allah loves people who please him," but there is a radical difference between saying "Allah loves" and "Allah *is* love." There is also no place in Judaism that you can find the statement "YHWH is love." Only when the doctrine of the Trinity is revealed can we truly understand the nature of our God: "God is love" (1 Jn 4:8). There must be more than one to have love. God is a self-contained unit, three in one, finding fulfillment in each other. God is love, because there are three persons in love with each other. We are single individuals, and so we must find our fulfillment outside of ourselves. The amazing truth is the invitation that we are given to be receivers of the triune Love and part of God's triune conversation.

Jeremiah 10:23 simply declares that "*adam*'s way is not in himself." Men and women need to receive life from him. If we try to play the God part, disaster will come. When we recognize his aseity (self-sufficiency) and our contingency (dependence on him), then we have the chance to find life, sustenance, explanation, and fulfillment. Our way is in him!

4
The Need for Holiness[1]

THE GOSPEL OF MARK

Papa had a remarkable experience of sanctification when he was thirteen at Indian Springs Holiness Camp Meeting under the preaching of Henry Clay Morrison. He believed that Christ could cleanse a human heart from self-interest through the gift of the Holy Spirit. Jeremiah 10:23 began his quest to understand how human persons were created so that they could receive the gift of the Spirit. The book of Mark provided a picture of fallen human nature and its dramatic turn towards self, even after encountering Christ. Jeremiah 10 tells us what we are made for; Mark tells us why we cannot get there on our own.

Papa's sermon on the Gospel of Mark gives a picture of hearts that have not been cleansed from self-interest. Papa believed that self-interest in a follower of Christ was the most destructive type of self-interest because it marred the witness of a Christian life. He believed that the experience of Pentecost was not simply a one-time historical event but the Father's means of filling all believers with the fullness of his triune life. He understood Pentecost to be primarily about the cleansing from self-interest and the receiving of the Holy Spirit to enable a human person to live in intimacy and freedom with the

---

1   This sermon also appears in *Discipleship: Essays in Honor of Dr. Allan Coppedge* (Telios Press and Francis Asbury Press, 2017), edited by Matt Friedeman.

Father and Christ Jesus. He did not believe it was intended primarily for power to do signs and wonders but to live full of the Spirit of Jesus.

The work of Samuel Logan Brengle became a key for Papa after his experience at Indian Springs. Brengle had experienced the same kind of cleansing love that Papa had found, and it became for Brengle as well as for Papa the foundation stone of his life. Brengle's writings helped Papa understand what it meant to live in continual intimacy with the triune God through the life of the Holy Spirit. This theological understanding of entire sanctification or the infilling of the Holy Spirit was never popular in Christian circles, and Papa encountered the opposition that resulted from this understanding of the gospel, as had Brengle. He never wavered, and I think his understanding of personhood helped him hold steady on this point. He believed that human persons were created to be fulfilled from an outside source, and that source is the life and person of the Holy Spirit.

"Who do people say I am?"
They replied, "Some say John the Baptist; others say Elijah; and still others, one of the prophets."
"But what about you?" he asked. "Who do you say I am?"
Peter answered, "You are the Messiah." (Mark 8:27–29)

One time when I was invited to speak in Asbury Theological Seminary's chapel, I considered what I would say to young men and women who were studying for the ministry that would be of profit to them. As I prayed about it, the burden that came to me was the matter of Christian discipleship. What is a disciple? Who is a disciple? What does it mean to be a disciple of Jesus Christ? To prepare myself for that assignment, I thought that I would take one of the Gospels and read it very carefully, working my way through one Gospel to see how Jesus dealt with the issue of discipleship, from the calling of his twelve disciples until the resurrection. I suppose I chose Mark because it was the shortest of the four Gospels. I wanted to be able to sit down and read it through from beginning to end at one sitting without stopping.

I wanted to get in my mind the content of that little book, particularly as it related to the subject of discipleship.

There is something beautiful about the way God will open up a verse so that it just stands out and one can say, "This is my verse for the day. This is my verse for the year. This is the word on which I live at this moment." It is an even better thing when a paragraph just comes alive and the parts of it all fit together. When one can understand a whole chapter, it is great, but when the whole structure of a biblical book can be seen, it is far greater and helps the reader see the world from God's perspective. All of us ought to work towards seeing the big pictures so that we can see things whole, because there are things that can be seen only when we look at the totality of the text that could never be seen clearly when we look at any one part.

As I worked my way through the book of Mark, I began to understand something of the sequence and logic of the book. In the process, two things stood out brilliantly and dramatically. The first one I had seen before, but it came home to me afresh. That is the beauty of Scripture; it keeps opening to us in deeper and deeper ways. Mark, in writing his Gospel, is concerned about one question: who is Jesus? In his opening paragraph, a group of Jews gather around John the Baptist with the question, "Is this the Christ?" John turns the attention from himself to Jesus. Jesus is the bridegroom and John simply bears witness to him. Carefully, deliberately, and dramatically, Mark builds his case to prove Jesus' identity as the Messiah. He is the one about whom John the Baptist said, "the straps of whose sandals I am not worthy to untie" (Jn 1:27).

Mark builds the suspense for eight chapters of his Gospel in good Hebrew fashion. There are many scholars who do not believe that each Gospel was written by a single author. They think rather that the Gospel stories are bits of tradition that were collected and somebody, perhaps not even an eyewitness, took these bits and pieces and put them together like beads on a string, so each Gospel is put together of various bits and pieces of stories from Jesus' life, but they are not whole units composed by single individuals. As I lived with the Gospel of Mark, the unity of the book became clearer and clearer, and the single authorship of it seemed obvious as the case unfolded to answer the question, "Who is Jesus?" Mark answers this question as powerfully as he can.

Mark does not make his case in the way a lawyer or a philosopher would do it. Our tendency is to take our basic principles and lay them down logically and build discursively until finally we can draw the conclusion that we think should be drawn from the data. That is not the way a good Hebrew did things. In fact, there is a vast difference in the way a Hebrew mind and a Greek mind works, and it is demonstrated in the way they would argue a case. When a person came to Jesus and asked him a question, he did not start into a logical discourse. Instead, he told a story. The Hebrew mind illustrated truth rather than rationally discussing it. Jesus painted a picture in the mind of his listeners that was better than a thousand logical discourses.

Mark begins to build his case, not discursively, but rather picture by picture by picture by picture. Each one is drawn to provoke the question, "Who is Jesus?" In his very first chapter, Mark just plunks the reader headlong into his argument. Jesus sits at the synagogue at Capernaum, he finds a man who has an unclean spirit, and he speaks to the man with the unclean spirit. The unclean spirit is expelled from him, and the man is set free. Then Jesus begins to teach the people who have gathered at the synagogue, and they are astounded, for they had never heard a man who spoke like Jesus. The people begin to ask the question, "Who is this man?"

After that visit to the synagogue, Jesus and his newfound disciples go with Peter to his home, and Peter's mother-in-law is sick with a fever. Jesus sees her and lays his hand upon her. The fever is driven away, and she is made well. She gets up and serves them, and one can imagine these disciples saying, "We knew John, and he was a great prophet, but he never did anything like this. It seems that no matter what the problem is, Jesus is the answer!"

Then before the disciples know what is happening, a man comes running to them and, to their astonishment and terror, he is a leper.

He does not, as a leper was supposed to, run in the other direction and say, "Unclean! Unclean!" He draws near to Jesus and falls on his knees in front of Jesus. I am confident that the disciples scattered, watching from a distance to see what Jesus would do. Jesus does the unthinkable and reaches out and lays his hand on the man. The leper is confident that Jesus has the authority to make him clean; he only wonders if Jesus *wants* to make him clean. Jesus does want to make him clean, so he touches the one no one else would touch, and the man is cleansed of his leprosy.

Then Mark paints another picture of the Sabbath day. Jesus is teaching and some men bring a paralytic to him. They lift the tiles from the roof, and he is lowered until he lies on the ground in front of Jesus. Unperturbed, Jesus looks at the paralytic and declares that his sins are forgiven. The Pharisees and the scribes are indignant and ask among themselves, "Why does this fellow talk like that? He's blaspheming! Who can forgive sins but God alone?" (Mk 2:7). Jesus knows their thoughts and responds to their anger with the power to forgive sins and heal the body. He instructs the man to get up and walk. He explains that he performed the miracle because, "I want you to know that the Son of Man has authority on earth to forgive sins. . ." (Mk 2:10).

Following this is the story of the man with the withered hand. Again, the Pharisees are watching to see if he will heal on the Sabbath. Jesus asks the man to hold out his hand, and as he does so his hand is made perfectly whole. The people go away wondering "Who is this man?" and "Where does he get his power?" Jesus stands in his hometown synagogue, and as he speaks the people watch him in awe. They know his family, his mother and brothers, and they cannot understand the source of his power and wisdom.

Mark continues his string of stories. One night the disciples are crossing the sea and a massive storm arises, and they come to Jesus who is sleeping in the boat and say, "Teacher, don't you care if we drown?" He simply arises, looks at the waves, turns to the wind, and says, "Quiet! Be still" (see Mk 4:38–39). The stormy night becomes instantly calm, but as the waves subside, a tempest begins inside the boat in the hearts and the minds of the disciples as they look at each other and wonder, "who is this man—a man that even the winds and waves obey?"

Through all Mark's stories, he is declaring to the reader that Jesus is perfectly able to meet every human need that arises. Never has there been a man like this man. He heals the sick, cleanses the leper, raises the paralytic, and calms the storm. There are a few parables that Mark records, but only a very few. Almost all of the first eight chapters of Mark give witness to the miraculous power of Christ to meet every human need. As each story is given, the disciples' or the crowd's reaction is recorded. The people wonder about his ability to forgive sins, they are confused by his healings on the Sabbath, they cannot understand his power over evil spirits, and they marvel at his ability to calm the storm. The Pharisees and the Herodians come together and declare that Jesus is dangerous and must be eliminated, but the common people listen to him and declare that he has done all things well (Mk 7:37). After this declaration, Jesus turns to his disciples and says:

> "Who do people say I am?"
> They replied, "Some say John the Baptist; others say Elijah; and still others, one of the prophets."
> "But what about you?" he asked. "Who do you say I am?"
> Peter answered, "You are the Messiah." (Mark 8:27–29)

This story is the climax of that first part of the book of Mark, halfway through the book. Jesus asks the ultimate question of every disciple-maker, "Who is Jesus?" Jesus has been with the disciples these three years, and they have had an opportunity to see him in all different situations with all different people. In that moment of illumination, Peter turns and says, "You are the Messiah." When Peter spoke, I am sure he spoke not only for himself but also for the eleven with him.

Mark does not linger or explain this pivotal moment in his book. He moves quickly and dramatically to the next big question; Mark is convinced that his readers understand who Jesus is. The first lesson is learned, and he wants to begin to answer the second question. I believe that the first step in being a disciple of Christ is to know who Christ is. No person will ever follow him fully until they have some grasp of who Jesus really is, and no person will ever give themselves totally, irrevocably, and completely to him until they know what Mark knew: that Jesus is the one who is sufficient for every human need. He is the all-sufficient One.

Immediately after that confession, a dramatic change occurs in the book. Before Peter's declaration, Mark has been telling these stories about who Jesus is. They have tumbled from him in quick succession, stacking up the data, but immediately after Peter's confession, the emphasis is different. Instead of an almost third-person atmosphere in which Jesus is detached from the twelve, performing his acts for their benefit as well as for others, now he reaches out his arms and draws the twelve into an intimacy with him that they have not known before. Now that they know him, his teaching begins. He begins to instruct them not in *who* he is but in *why* he came. Now that they know who he is, he wants them to know what is going to happen to him. He lets them know that they will go to Jerusalem, and his enemies will make him suffer; they will beat him and crucify him. He will die. Peter takes him aside and rebukes him. Jesus is now introducing them into the mystery of his mission, and Peter cannot comprehend or else cannot bear to hear it. Jesus looks at him and says, "Get behind me, Satan! . . . You do not have in mind the concerns of God, but merely human concerns" (Mk 8:33).

Jesus continues his teaching by taking three of his disciples up on a mountain and, when he gets them up on a mountain, he is transfigured before Peter, James, and John. He is transfigured before them and to their astonishment, awe, and (I am sure) terror, they look and see Moses and Elijah standing with Jesus—Moses, the architect of Israel's religion, that man who talked face to face with God and did not die and Elijah, that stormy old prophet, who brought God's word to the nation of Israel and was carried to heaven in a chariot of fire.

To their amazement, Moses and Elijah talk with Jesus, and it is crystal clear to Peter, James, and John that Jesus is greater than even Moses and Elijah, the two greatest prophets in Israel's history. All that they had confessed about Jesus is true: he is the Holy One of God, the Son of God, the Christ, the Messiah, the Savior.

Now the disciples are on the inside of the secret of Jesus' identity. As they start down the mountain, Jesus again tells them what is going to happen. He tells them that he must go to Jerusalem, suffer, and die, but he also tells them that he will rise from the dead. Then he instructs them not to tell anyone about the Transfiguration until he has risen from the dead. Just like a bunch of systematic theologians, the disciples huddle up and discuss what "rising from the dead" could possibly mean. When they get to the foot of the hill, there is a great commotion. Jesus walks straight into the commotion and finds that his other nine disciples are at the heart of it. He asks the crowd about the problem. A troubled man comes and says, "Teacher, I brought you my son, who is possessed by a spirit that has robbed him of speech. Whenever it seizes him, it throws him to the ground. . . . I asked your disciples to drive out the spirit, but they could not" (Mk 9:17–18).

Jesus replies, "You unbelieving generation . . . how long shall I stay with you? How long shall I put up with you? Bring the boy to me" (Mk 9:19). The father brings his son, and his son is set free and healed.

Notice how these three stories after Peter's declaration answer a completely different set of questions with a completely different set of stories. Instead of stories about dramatic acts of Christ and his adequacy, Jesus tells Peter, "Get behind me, Satan!" (Mk 8:33). To the three on the Mount of Transfiguration, he tries to explain to them what it meant for the Son of Man to be rejected. To the disciples confronted by the spirit-possessed boy, Jesus calls them, "unbelieving generation" (Mk 9:19). They are confused and afraid about the message of his mission.

Their consternation continues as they walk down through Galilee toward Jerusalem. They come to the end of the day when Jesus turns to his disciples and says, "What were you arguing about on the road?"

(Mk 9:33). They look at each other and blush, and Peter, so eager to speak before, now is strangely silent. James and John, intimate in the deeper things, look at each other and have nothing to say. Jesus knows what they were discussing; they were talking about who would be the greatest in Jesus' kingdom. While Jesus is going to Jerusalem to a cross, they are looking for a way to get a throne and a crown.

The disciples' performance gets even worse. They come to Jesus for approval after forbidding a man to cast out demons in Jesus' name. Jesus rebukes them and declares that those who are not against him are for him. Jesus knows that any man who meets a human need in Jesus' name is not an enemy.

They bring children to Jesus, and the disciples tell the parents to take them away, declaring that Jesus does not have time for children. Jesus rebukes them and says, "Let the little children come to me, and do not hinder them, for the kingdom of God belongs to such as these" (Mk 10:14). James and John ask Jesus, "Let one of us sit at your right and the other at your left in your glory" (Mk 10:37). He says, "You don't know what are asking. . . . Can you drink the cup I drink or be baptized with the baptism I am baptized with?" (Mk 10:39). Then he explains that they will drink the cup of suffering that he will drink, but they do not understand. Jesus turns and says to them that all of them will forsake him, and although they all deny that they will abandon him, that is exactly what happens in the Garden of Gethsemane.

The difference in the stories in Mark is amazing. In eight chapters, Jesus demonstrates his *adequacy*, and then for seven and a half long chapters the disciples demonstrate their *inadequacy*. There is little discussion of their inadequacy until they come to believe that Jesus is the Christ. No person will ever know his own sinfulness and inadequacy until he comes to saving faith.

I am firmly convinced that the first step in discipleship is to know who Jesus is, and the second step in discipleship is to find out who we are. We must understand that he is enough for every situation, and then we must recognize our inability to meet the needs of human life.

No human flesh will be able to boast in itself. It is not what we do that has significance; it is only what he does.

Mark drives this lesson home with the story of the Transfiguration. Why does he name Peter, James, and John when Jesus takes them up on the mountain? I think he wants us to see clearly the three best of his disciples. It was these disciples who asked for the best seats in his kingdom but who denied him and fled from him when the soldiers came to arrest him later in the Garden of Gethsemane. Mark names Peter at the denial of Jesus in order to press home the point that all of the disciples had the same problem—the same problem as all of us. There are no exceptions. The best among us are no better than the worst. The strongest are no better than the weakest, and Peter failed just like all the rest. The very best of the flesh is not enough. Mark even goes so far as to include the detail about the young man in the linen cloth who flees naked from the soldiers in Gethsemane. Tradition holds that the young man was Mark himself. Mark wants to be sure his readers know that he is no exception; he flees just like all the disciples (see Mk 14:51–52). When the resurrection comes, two points are crystal clear: the complete adequacy of the Savior and the total inadequacy of his disciples.

If the story had stopped there, Mark would be a rather miserable book, but it does not stop there; Mark sets the scene, and the other Gospels and Acts finish it. Luke tells about how the disciples go to Jerusalem, and after Jesus ascends, they meet in an upper room for prayer and confession, intercession and repentance. Having now seen themselves clearly, I am sure they recount all the events in Mark's Gospel with a sense of their own inadequacy and sin. On the tenth day, the Holy Spirit comes, anoints them, and fills them, and after that, they suddenly understand the cross and the resurrection. When people turn and begin to ask questions, Peter, whose denial was more pointed than any other disciple, stands up and explains the purpose of Jesus' death and resurrection. The one whose understanding has been so dim blazes forth with the Spirit of God. For the first time, he can really see and understand. Filled with the Spirit, the disciples are ready to take the Kingdom to the world in the name of the Savior. They are powerless in their own human flesh, and they are now aware of that powerlessness, but now they also know Christ's resurrection power. Going into the temple they meet a beggar and they say, "Silver or gold I do not have, but what I do have I give you. In the name of Jesus Christ of Nazareth, walk" (Acts 3:6). Impotence becomes power through the gift of the Holy Spirit.

The carnal spirit has been cleansed and has now become one of sacrificial devotion. Before the resurrection and the infilling of the Holy Spirit, the disciples all forsake him. In Acts 4, the disciples look into the faces of the people who crucified Jesus and without fear say, "Which is right in God's eyes: to listen to you, or to him? You be the judges! As for us, we cannot help speaking about what we have seen and heard" (Acts 4:19–20). Fear gives way to the courage of the Holy Spirit.

The reader may ask why Mark did not record the dramatic change that occurs after the resurrection and the giving of the Holy Spirit. That is the question that came to my mind. Why is Mark so incomplete? Then I realized Mark is not incomplete. In the opening paragraph of Mark, John the Baptist states, "After me comes the one more powerful than I, the straps of whose sandals I am not worthy to stoop down and untie. I baptize you with water, but he will baptize you with the Holy Spirit" (Mk 1:7–8). Then Mark records Jesus' baptism and the coming of the Holy Spirit on Jesus. "Just as Jesus was coming up out of the water, he saw heaven being torn open and the Spirit descending on him like a dove. And a voice came from heaven: 'You are my Son, whom I love; with you I am well pleased'" (Mk 1:10–11). In the opening paragraph of Mark, he spells out the answer to the basic problem of discipleship that the book displays so dramatically.

Do you understand why we talk about the need for the infilling of the Holy Spirit? After a person has been converted, he must come to know who the Messiah is and who he is, and then he must experience the fullness of God's living, quickening Spirit within. No person is adequate until there has been in his or her life a personal Pentecost.

Thursday night before the cross, Jesus and his disciples are in the upper room. He is talking personally with his twelve disciples. It is the scene of greatest intimacy between the disciples and Jesus that the Gospels record, and what does Jesus say? "I will ask the Father, and he will give you another advocate to help you and be with you forever—the Spirit of truth. . ." (Jn 14:16–17). Jesus knew he had to leave his disciples, but he also knew the Father would send One to take his place. He instructs his disciples to wait for him in Jerusalem until he comes. The disciples have loved Jesus and found him to be adequate for every need, and now they will be given the Spirit of Jesus so that his adequacy can be within them.

Let me ask you, have you had John the Baptist's promise fulfilled in your life? "He will baptize you with the Holy Spirit" (Mk 1:8). What's the proof of the baptism of the Holy Spirit? It is the end of our own self-will and our attempts to meet the needs of the world on our own. It is the cross! As we die to our own will, we begin to know the Spirit's divine power. We begin to live as true disciples of Jesus Christ, filled with his Spirit and sharing his love.

5
Is Jesus Lord?

Psalm 16

I heard this sermon from Papa when I was in high school. I never forgot its impact on me. This sermon seemed to be the testimony of my grandfather's life. The psalm itself is set up as a witness. It begins with a cry for help and ends with a prophecy of the promised Messiah. It begins with "me" and ends with Jesus. When Papa would read this psalm, it would be as if he were giving witness to what happens when we make Jesus Lord of our lives. As his grandchildren, we found it easy to trust Christ because of Papa's witness. He made it seem like the happiest thing in the world.

Papa was thirteen when he became a believer at Indian Springs Holiness Camp Meeting. He had a Bible teacher, Mother Clark, who asked him one day if he would help her carry her things to her room. Flattered, he said he would and on the way she asked if he was a Christian. Without hesitation, he honestly said, "No." Then without much fanfare, she introduced him to Jesus in such a way that his heart was overflowing with love. It was three days later, in the main tabernacle, that my grandfather heard Henry Clay Morrison speak on full surrender. Papa went to the altar, and he experienced the love of Jesus so profoundly that it became the defining moment of his life, the moment when he made Jesus Lord of his life.

His sermon on the Gospel of Mark spells out our need for holiness and the infilling of the Holy Spirit; his sermon on Psalm 16 gives the Old Testament witness to this reality. It is possible for Christ to be that which our souls desire and the One in whom our souls take refuge.

As the psalmist declares, "You are my Lord; apart from you I have no good thing" (Ps 16:2). Papa found the goodness of God and did not let it go. He was convinced of that goodness until the very end of his life, and he would regularly say to visitors and family, "I am the richest man in the world." That was his testimony to God's goodness to him.

The end of this psalm is about the coming Christ, and the end of Papa's life was about Jesus. Worship was the regular theme coming from the back bedroom in which he spent most of his time near the end of his life. He taught me that Scripture produces worship, music produces worship, family produces worship, and even politics produces worship. He said to me, "Cricket, pray with me that Jesus would get the center stage! The day is going to come when every knee will bow and every tongue will confess."

Psalm 16:9–11 could be Papa's final witness: "Therefore my heart is glad and my tongue rejoices; my body also will rest secure, because you will not abandon me to the realm of the dead, nor will you let your faithful one see decay. You make known to me the path of life; you will fill me with joy in your presence, with eternal pleasures at your right hand."

Keep me safe, my God, for in you I take refuge.
I say to the Lord, "You are my Lord; apart from you I have no good thing." I say of the holy people who are in the land, "They are the noble ones in whom is all my delight." Those who run after other gods will suffer more and more. I will not pour out libations of blood to such gods or take up their names on my lips.
Lord, you alone are my portion and my cup; you make my lot secure. The boundary lines have fallen for me in pleasant places; surely I have a delightful inheritance. I will

praise the LORD, *who counsels me; even at night my heart instructs me. I keep my eyes always on the* LORD. *With him at my right hand, I will not be shaken.*

Therefore my heart is glad and my tongue rejoices; my body also will rest secure, because you will not abandon me to the realm of the dead, nor will you let your faithful one see decay. You make known to me the path of life; you will fill me with joy in your presence, with eternal pleasures at your right hand. (Psalm 16)

What does it mean to be holy? In my opinion, Psalm 16 is the most precious and the clearest testimony in all of Scripture about a holy life. One of the things that impresses me is that it was written before Christ, possibly a thousand years before Christ. We tend to think of holiness as a New Testament doctrine, connected with Pentecost. I challenge you to look at this psalm as a clear picture of God's intention that his people be a holy people.

What does it mean to be a holy people? To answer that question, we must look at Jesus, the Holy One. How did he understand his own identity? The first time Jesus came to Jerusalem after he had been presented to Israel by John the Baptist, he went immediately to the temple. The last time Jesus went to the city of Jerusalem before his crucifixion, he returned to the temple. On both occasions, he cleansed it, driving out the moneychangers. In dramatic fashion, he explained to Jerusalem who he really was. The temple was built for him, the Lord of all creation. He had come to his own house, and his own people did not receive him. At the beginning and at the end of his ministry, he asserted his Lordship as well as his deity. Jesus was Lord of the house, and his own people chose to reject him. When Christ comes to us, he can only come as Lord because that is who he is. It would be a lie and a delusion if he allowed us to believe he was anyone but Lord and Master. Becoming a Christian means that we acknowledge who Christ really is. He is the Lord!

In the first century, the Lordship of Jesus became the touchstone of what it meant to be a Christian. Paul wrote to the Roman Church and clearly explained the heart of the Good News, that if believers confess with their lips that Jesus is Lord and believe in their hearts that God has raised him from the dead, they will be saved (Rom 10:9). The affirmation that Jesus is Lord and the belief that the resurrection really happened is the heart of our salvation.

Philippians 2 contains a passage about the mind of Christ. Some scholars think that Paul was quoting an early Christian hymn about how Christ humbled himself, emptied himself, and became human even to the point of death. God has highly exalted Christ and given him a name which is above every name, a name at which every knee shall bow and ultimately everyone shall confess that Jesus Christ is Lord to the glory of God the Father.

The Christian is the person who confesses Jesus as Lord now, because everybody else will confess it then. It is not a question of whether we will acknowledge his Lordship, it is simply of *when* we will acknowledge it. Will we acknowledge it when all creation acknowledges it? It will have no saving power in that day. When we acknowledge Jesus as Lord, even though the world denies it, it has dramatic transforming power. In 1 Corinthians 12, Paul writes, "Now about the gifts of the Spirit, brothers and sisters, I do not want you to be uninformed. You know that when you were pagans, somehow or other you were influenced and led astray to mute idols. Therefore I want you to know that no one who is speaking by the Spirit of God says, 'Jesus be cursed,' and no one can say, 'Jesus is Lord,' except by the Holy Spirit" (1 Cor 12:1–3).

The world is always present with us, and its pressures are great. The sinfulness of our hearts is strong enough that no one will ever make Jesus Lord without divine help. Your heart will wander; my heart will wander. Every heart will follow the crowd unless there is divine power that comes to us, that enables us to say, "No, I don't believe that is the thing to which I want to give my life. I believe Jesus is the One to whom I must give my life."

There is a story from the early Church that I have always loved about a wisp of a girl. I have always imagined she was in her teens from the way the story has been transmitted. She was in the arena, ready to be sacrificed to the lions because she was a Christian. The story is told that a Roman senator noticed her. He was so moved by this innocent and helpless girl standing there, ready to be fed to the wild beasts, that he came and looked at her and said, "Why do you have to do it? All you have to do is pour three drops of oil and speak three words, 'Caesar is Lord,' and your life is saved." We can imagine what went on in his head. "Surely there is no God in all creation that would ever ask this little one to forfeit her life when three short words would save it. Why, she could spend the rest of her life living out her faith. How long would it take her to say those three little words? Is your God so exhausting in his claim on you, that you can't steal three seconds to save your life?" That is how the world thinks. She looked back at him and said, "Sir, Caesar isn't Lord."

In one last attempt, he said, "Daughter, do you hear those lions?"

She turned her head to listen as if that was a new thought. Then she looked at him and said, "Yes, I do. But sir, do you hear the angels?" It is the Spirit of God in a person's heart that enables one to stand against the spirit of the age.

Why is it necessary? Simply to be different or to combat the spirit of the times? No, it is for the same reason that Jesus was filled with the Spirit before he began his ministry, so that the world, which does not understand, can be saved. The world will never be saved if we capitulate to it, but if we let his Spirit fill us, then we can stand and be a redemptive agent in a world that is bound and an instrument of light in a world that is lost.

One of the best passages that I have found anywhere in Scripture to spell out what it means for Christ to be Lord does not come after Christ but before him. It is in the Old Testament, in Psalm 16. This psalm is a specific testimony, perhaps written a thousand years before Christ. I have come to love that fact, because the eternal God never changes his nature, his provisions, or his demands. The Lord God was Lord a thousand years before Christ as much as he is Lord today, and the psalmist saw it and recorded it for us. I would like to go through that psalm, step by step, and bear witness with the psalmist as to what it means for a person to make God Lord in his life.

The psalm begins, "Keep me safe, my God, for in you I take refuge." I love the fact that many of the psalms begin with their conclusion. The psalms flow out of the psalmist's experience, and they are his witness. The Hebrew does not contain the word "safe." It is simply "Keep me, O God." This is the psalmist's conclusion, for he has come to know that there is no way that he can be what he is supposed to be apart from the gracious gift of God. Unholy people like you and me can never become holy except through God's divine redemption, his divine work within our hearts, and if we ever get to the point where our hearts are clean, the only way they will ever stay clean is for him to keep our hearts. No human person can keep their own heart. Only God can keep a human heart clean and free.

"I say to the Lord, you are my Lord . . ." (Ps 16:2). When the word *LORD* is written in capitals, it indicates the personal name of God in the Old Testament. It is the Old Testament counterpart to *Jesus*. It is the name *Yahweh*, the personal name of the God of Israel. The first Lord in your text is a personal name, and then comes the affirmation that YHWH is Lord.

Notice how the psalmist defines what it means for YHWH to be Lord: "apart from you I have no good thing" (Ps 16:2). The Hebrew is more cryptic than the English. It literally says, "my good, not, beside you." The psalmist declares that there is no good for him separated from YHWH and his will for the psalmist. That is particularly interesting in the Old Testament, because the Old Testament teaches a doctrine of *creatio ex nihilo*, that God created everything out of nothing. Everything that exists is originally good. The writer looks around at a world that God has created; it is good because of the goodness of God. The goodness in anything is drawn from its relationship to the Lord God and from the fact that it is his will for you. In the last line of the psalm he says, "you will fill me with joy in your presence, with eternal pleasures at your right hand" (Ps 16:11). The psalmist knows that God's right hand is full of good things, and he is not going to seek anything else in the world except what God has in his right hand. No matter how good anything is, if it is not in God's right hand for me, it will not be good for me. It may be good for my neighbor, it may be good for somebody else, but there is nothing good for me if it is not in his plan for me. I will let him determine what should be in my life.

This choice to let YHWH determine what is good for one's life splits the world up into two groups of people, and the writer identifies those two groups of people. The first group is the saints. "I say of the holy people who are in the land, 'They are the noble ones in whom is all my delight'" (Ps 16:3). This psalm anticipates the New Testament at this point because the word that is used for "saints" is a word that is not used in the Old Testament often for a simple believer. Its Greek counterpart is the most common word used in the New Testament for a Christian (*hagias*), "a holy one." In the Old Testament, *quadesh* (holy) is normally used to describe Yahweh and only occasionally applied to people. It is used for the Levites who served in the temple and for Aaron as the one who walked into the Holy of Holies once a year. It is also used for a prophet in 2 Kings, a man who bore the Word of God. Psalm 16 uses it for the people who say, "Yahweh is Lord." They are the "holy ones." They have put him first and made him Lord, and the result is that his character has come to them and they have become remarkably like him. The psalmist says, "I see the holy ones, the ones that belong wholly and only to him." One of the marks of a holy person is one in whom God takes delight.

One group is composed of the holy ones, the ones who have recognized him as Lord and made him Lord in their lives. The second group is those who run after something else. "Those who run after other gods will suffer more and more. . . " (Ps 16:4). The Hebrew simply states, "those who hasten after another multiply their sorrow." Every idol is ultimately a creature of one kind or another. All the gods in the Ancient World were created forces; in our day, an idol may be a vocation, a human being, a position in life, an ambition, or satisfaction of our own desires. The only options for ultimate reality in our lives are God or part of his creation. When we put a part of God's creation ahead of God himself, we corrupt it. All of God's creation is good, but the moment it becomes lord in our lives, it becomes evil and destructive. God insists that he be Lord in our lives not because he wants to control us but because he *is* Lord, and our lives need to match reality. If they do, they can be clean, healthy, and wholesome. Holiness and wholeness go together because when God is first, everything else works as it is supposed to work.

Genesis 3, Eve's story, throws some light on the suffering that comes to those who follow other gods. She has no intention of losing the garden or of losing her relationship with God, but a beautiful piece of fruit attracts her notice, and she listens to a slander against God. She knows the fruit will be sweet to the taste and that it will make her wise, more experienced. She decides to take the fruit and try to keep God's presence and provision, too. She does not realize that when she chooses one, she sacrifices the other. When we put anything else in Christ's place and make it our objective, we immediately corrupt our relationship with him. God's punishment for Eve fits with this reality; her greatest moment of joy and fulfillment, childbearing, becomes marked by great pain. In the same way, pain comes into the life of the person because he puts something ahead of God in his life. His natural habitat, which has been good and refreshing to him, becomes hostile. Whenever we want to hold on to Christ and something else, we find that we lose him, and what we held onto becomes corrupted and corrupting. Anything in human life that is placed ahead of him will damage you and you will damage it, including relationships with those whom you love most.

"I will not pour out libations of blood to such gods or take up their names on my lips (Ps 16:4). When I first starting working with this psalm, I glossed over this section, thinking that it only applied in the Old Testament. It seemed to have no application for me, but then I realized that was simply because I was unfamiliar with the language of the text. In the Old Testament, the priests pour out liquid offerings to the Lord: blood, oil, water, or wine. We talk about someone who "pours out his life for others." This psalmist declares that he will not pour out his life in the way his neighbors do for the idols. He will save his life for the Lord and pour it out for him.

Paul understands this idea of pouring his life out as a drink offering to the Lord. In Philippians 2:17, he says, "Even if I am to be poured out as a drink offering upon the sacrificial offering of your faith, I am glad and rejoice with you all" (ESV). He knew that his life was to be spilled out for Christ. We are going to pour our lives out for something—either ourselves, or our idols, or Jesus. When we make Jesus Lord, our lives will flow out for him, but if we choose not to make him Lord, we can count on pain and travail, tension and hostility, loneliness and death. This is the biblical story.

The psalmist says, "I will not . . . take up their names on my lips" (Ps 16:4). Our speech reflects who is Lord. Talking religiously does not mean that Jesus is Lord in our lives, but when we get him as Lord, our speech will be different and our words will reflect who sits on the throne of our lives. A relatively young Christian told me with joy about the new things God was revealing to her. She delighted in his ways even though some of those ways were causing unrest and change in her heart and life. I found it very telling when she said, "When I try to talk about them with other people, they just don't seem interested." Let me have a record of your conversations when you are talking with your closest friend, your roommate, or a family member and I will tell you who sits on the throne of your heart.

"Lord, you alone are my portion and my cup . . ." (Ps 16:5). *He* is what I am going to eat and drink. This is the Old Testament's counterpart to the Lord's Supper. The reason most of us are afraid to take our hands off our lives and let Christ have total control is that we are scared something bad will happen. We get uneasy about the security of the future when we take our hands off our lives. The first thing the psalmist says is that YHWH has made his lot secure, and he is in an unshaken place because God is always at his right hand.

When you allow Christ to captain the boat, the storm does not matter. He is the one who in charge of all the storms. He can speak one word, and the storms will cease. Why do we believe that we will be less secure with Jesus in control of our lives? It is because we have a perverted, twisted notion of who Jesus is. If we know Jesus as Lord, we recognize that we are safest when we are in the center of his will. If I take my hands off my life and let Christ have it, he will take care of his own.

Do you know what Jesus said about his disciples when the soldiers came to arrest him? He turned to the Roman soldiers and the temple police and he said, "Let these men go" (Jn 18:8). Jesus did not intend to lose one of those who belong to him—except for Judas, who made his own choice. He will keep you if you keep to him. He is your security.

When I came to the question of the Lordship of Christ over my life, whether I would be wholly his, I kept thinking, "What will I lose if let him run my life?" We are so sinful that we never think about what we will gain when we make him Lord—we are always afraid of losing. The psalmist says, "You make my lot secure" (Ps 16:5). God says to his people, "There you stand at the gambling table, and your life is on the line. Are you going to roll the dice or trust me with control?" The psalmist commits his lot to the Lord, and the result is happiness.

"The boundary lines have fallen for me in pleasant places . . ." (Ps 16:6). The psalmist lets the Lord draw the lines on his life, and he finds the portion that comes to him exceedingly pleasant. I can bear witness with the psalmist to this truth. I became a Christian when I was thirteen. I came to Indian Springs Holiness Camp Meeting and heard the message of holiness of heart. Something within me responded, and I knew I wanted him to be Lord. If I had ever had the vaguest dream of how good he wanted to be to me, I would have lived closer to him, and I would have been a more enthusiastic disciple and follower. His dream for you is infinitely better than anything you are ever going to dream. He loves you and wants you to be happy more than you do, and best of all he knows what you need to complete your life, fulfill it, and make it joyous. "I have a delightful inheritance" (Ps 16:6). What he is given is good, and what is coming is even better since I have made him Lord.

Because of this confidence in the one who holds his course and his future, the psalmist declares, "I will praise the LORD, who counsels me . . ." (Ps 16:7). We commonly think that we will know his will for us and then have an option to either accept it or reject it, but the truth is we do not know his will for us until we make him Lord. His will and perfect plan come to those who put him first; otherwise, even his will can be a substitute for his presence. God does not want you to choose his will; God wants you to choose him, and then he will disclose his will to you.

"I will praise the LORD, who counsels me; even at night my heart instructs me. I keep my eyes always on the LORD. With him at my right hand, I will not be shaken. Therefore my heart is glad and my tongue rejoices; my body also will rest secure" (Ps 16:7–9). That is an astounding verse from the Old Testament. The psalmist joyfully proclaims that having God as Lord is not only good spiritually but also good physically. The ancient world had no certainty about life after death, but the psalmist declared that the One to whom he had entrusted his life would be his security after death. He knew that God would not let death be the end of him because of God's love for him. His belief in life after death came out of the personal relationship to the God that he believed loved him enough that he would not let him go. He would want to keep him in his presence. God loves you enough that he wants eternal fellowship with you, and when death comes for those who have made him Lord, it will simply be a moment of transition, and after that you will find yourself in him.

"You will not abandon me to the realm of the dead, nor will you let your faithful one see decay. You make known to me the path of life; you will fill me with joy in your presence, with eternal pleasures at your right hand" (Ps 16:10–11). What a conclusion!

What does it mean to make Christ Lord? It means that Christ becomes the way forward, and we live in his presence. Remember when the king of Babylon looked into the fiery furnace in which he had thrown the faithful men and said, "Weren't there three men that we tied up and threw into the fire? . . . Look! I see four men walking around in the fire, unbound and unharmed, and the fourth looks like a son of the gods" (Dan 3:24–25). I have always thought Shadrach, Meschach, and Abendego might have looked out of the fire and waved at the king at that moment. The Son of God's presence can turn a furnace into heaven. His presence can turn distress into joy, and without his presence, life's richest moments are empty.

When we make Christ Lord, we receive his presence, his goodness, and his plan. Then we can anticipate the future with joy and expectation. The person who turns his life totally over to God walks with a lilt in his step, a light in his eye, and a deathlessness in his existence that nobody else ever has. Is Jesus Lord in your life?

6

Walking by Faith

GENESIS 12:1-3

This sermon gives a beautiful description of what a fully surrendered life looks like. Holiness simply means attaching oneself to Christ and detaching oneself from all other things. Like Paul in the New Testament, Papa consistently came back to Abraham as the model for what following Christ really is supposed to be. Papa's life mirrored Abraham's in some ways: God was continually calling him to journey out and trust God in new and unexpected ways. God called Papa to leave the pastorate in North Carolina and to go to school; he left one school and began to pastor an independent church in Loudonville, New York; he left a beloved church to teach Hebrew at Asbury Theological Seminary; he left a job he loved as a professor to become president of Asbury College; he left Asbury College to help raise up the local Church to support institutions like Asbury for future generations. When God said "Go!" Papa was willing to move, even if it meant leaving security and fulfillment. God was faithful to Papa, as he was to Abraham. He keeps his promises when his people are willing to follow him.

Some of our family's most cherished moments have come from listening to Papa recount God's faithful answers to prayer. I remember as a young college student walking into my grandparents' house and realizing a party was going on with just my grandmother and my grandfather. They had been praying for funding to help international Christian leaders attend Asbury College and Seminary to receive the training they needed to return to Eastern Europe and share Jesus. Papa had just ended a phone conversation in which enough money was given to keep these students in school. In my mind, it was an exceedingly large amount of money. As I watched them celebrate and entered into their joy, I knew that they had trusted God on behalf of these students, and God had heard their prayers and had been faithful to answer his promise of provision.

This was not an isolated instance. Consistently, God was faithful to provide for them as they trusted him with their finances, their family, their calling, their ministry, and their relationship. Their life verse was Matthew 6:33, "Seek ye first the kingdom of God and all these things shall be added unto you." As their family, we were able to watch God faithfully add all these things to our grandparents as they sought first God and his priorities.

This particular sermon is rich in illustrations, and the stories Papa uses to illustrate the scripture are from Henry Clay Morrison. Papa was sanctified under Henry Clay Morrison's preaching. He attended Asbury College as Morrison was ending his tenure there and founding Asbury Theological Seminary. Papa stood guard at Morrison's funeral service and felt the mantle of his leadership fall on him when he became president of Asbury College in 1968. One of Morrison's illustrations is about Abraham's baby buggy, which he purchased in hope of the baby who would be born to him and to Sarah. As a gift, someone gave Papa a baby buggy, which sits on his bookshelf even now. It is a testimony to our whole family of the faith that follows Christ and believes that all God's promises will be fulfilled. We live and we wait in joyful anticipation of the answers to promises that are coming.

The Lord had said to Abram, "Go from your country, your people and your father's household to the land I will show you.

"I will make you a great nation, and I will bless you; I will make your name great, and you will be a blessing. I will bless those who bless you, and whoever curses you I will curse; and all the peoples on earth will be blessed through you." (Genesis 12:1–3)

The eleventh chapter of Hebrews gives the roll call of the heroes of the faith. Surprisingly, almost twice as much space is devoted to Abraham as to anyone else. Not even Moses gets the attention that Abraham does, and I could make an easy case that Moses was the greatest man outside of Christ who ever lived. Despite Moses' greatness, Abraham is presented as the model for Christians. In God's wisdom, he made the first major character in Scripture the model for the rest of us. Abraham's story lets us know that the basic pattern of living by faith does not change. Abraham's life of faith is the pattern for all of us.

Sometimes I forget how early Abraham comes along. In Abraham's day, there are no Ten Commandments. That does not mean that Abraham is an immoral man, but Sinai and the giving of God's law have not yet occurred. In fact, it is not to come for centuries. In Abraham's time, there is no Church, so the worship of the true God is not institutionalized. The marks of faith that are so common to believers now have no part in his daily life. When Abraham follows God's call, no rituals or liturgy like sacraments or baptism exist. These symbols come later, but they are not a part of his life when he hears and answers the call of God.

I can see the divine wisdom in how God begins his story because it lets us know that law, the Church, and liturgy are not the essence of the gospel. These are not the heart of what God wants out of his followers. Of course, there is no question about the importance of the law; the law is God's standard of righteousness. God makes moral and ethical demands upon his people that they must obey. We come to live within the institutional expression of Christian faith, and we ought to be participants in and supporters of the Church; we need to feel an identity with it and promote it. And certainly, we should appreciate the sacraments, those visible symbols of our faith. Ultimately, however, the law, the Church, and the rituals are secondary to God's main purpose.

Sometimes I think of God's plan like this: I fell in love with Elsie, not with the institution of marriage. When we got ready to get married, people began to give us books. I found all sorts of books on marriage, but I never found a single book on Elsie. It was not marriage that I was after; it was Elsie. That is the way it was for fifty-nine years. Through those years, the one I wanted, the center of that life, was not a perfect marriage or the institution of marriage or the patterns established for it; it was simply Elsie.

God wants this kind of relationship with us, and so he gives Abraham as the model. He just says to him one day, "Follow me." That is basically what I said to Elsie, "Would you give up your home and a career to tag along with me? I like you, and my life will be so much richer if you go along with me, and from what I know, I'll be so much better if you'll go with me." Time has certainly vindicated that.

God's call to Abraham is just that simple. God says to Abraham "Go from your country, your people and your father's household to the land I will show you" (Gen 12:1). God wants Abraham to forsake all and attach himself to God—not to an institution or to a moral code or to any liturgy or ritual. God invites Abraham into a personal relationship with the living God. God calls Abraham to leave all that he had known and embark on an adventure following God himself. Any commitment of this magnitude to a person has certain costs that accompany it. God wants Abraham to attach himself to God alone, which means he had to detach from many other things. This is the reason that the Bible is so strong against idolatry: no one can attach his or her heart to two gods at the same time.

What are the things that Abraham had to detach from in order to attach himself to God? They are reflected in Genesis 12:1, where God says, "Go from your country, your people and your father's household . . ." These relationships form the normal social and cultural relationships of that time. It is significant to me that the first thing God says to Abraham is to leave his country. Our nationality is where many of our securities and much of our identity comes from. God wants our security to be in himself alone and in our relationship with him.

I suspect that Abraham thought twice about leaving his country. Ur was a center of great culture in that day; it was a very sophisticated city. We have artifacts from Ur during that period, and they are very beautiful things. It was a culture marked by aesthetic and economic wealth. It was also a culture marked by a very high standard of living. God called Abraham to leave all of that behind him. This is applicable to all of us who live in the Western world because we live in the most privileged position and culture in the world. It is in a culture like ours that God says to Abraham, "I want to be more important to you than your culture and all of its claims upon you." The place where God takes him was to the backwoods of nowhere, although God's promises to him were as big as the world itself. Abraham willingly left his culture behind to go where God called him to go.

I found myself sitting in the office of the Minister of Culture and Cults in Russia when it was under Communist rule. I knew it was going to be an incredibly hostile hour, and I could feel the apprehension in the Baptist pastors that went in with us. As their apprehension level went up, something inside me said, "Kinlaw, you're a long way from home." For me, America and Wilmore, Kentucky, meant security and identity, both which seemed so far away to me at that moment. God asked Abraham to put him above the land and culture to which he belonged. Do you have the kind of personal relationship with Christ that you are willing to give up your standard of living or your security for him? That is exactly what he asked the first person of major significance in the Bible to do.

God next asks Abraham to surrender his "people." Our people groups are another source of identity and security, perhaps even on a more intimate level than our country. I am very grateful that when I first became a Christian, God called me to break out of my social milieu. I grew up in a small town in North Carolina that had three textile mill villages around it. The social chasm between the town and the mill villages was like that between the Jews and the Samaritans. When I went to the first grade, there was a 1-A elementary and a 1-B elementary. The 1-A was the town kids, and 1-B was the mill kids. I never even met a mill kid until I was in the eighth grade even though we played on the same playground. We were never allowed to play together. When I was in high school, I started to break out of my social setting when I dated a girl from the B section; everybody in town was upset and concerned.

When I found Christ, I could not find a single person in my social group that was a born-again Christian. I searched to find somebody who knew the One that I knew, and I finally found two fellows from the mill village. One was an incredibly husky fellow and the other was very tall, with white kinky hair. Neither one were from the socially acceptable crowd. I did not earn any social prestige from aligning myself with these two believers, but I found that they loved Christ like I did. That was liberation for me, because I found that there are certain things that are infinitely more important than the things that our world values.

God puts Abraham, the first man in the Bible, through all of that, and then he asks for one more thing. He asks Abraham to leave his father and his mother and to walk with him. This is the kind of claim God makes on those he calls to himself. The end of the Bible is the story of all the nations of the earth coming to Christ; the beginning of the Bible is about one man being stripped of his ultimate allegiance to his own nation. I love the international nature of Scripture because God is building a kingdom bigger than any of our groups and bigger than any of our normal loyalties.

One of the things that I love is that when Christ asks us to surrender certain things, he always gives back more than he asks. You cannot out-give our God. He always gives in amazingly creative ways. He takes Abraham away from his family, but he gives him a family in return. Abraham does not think that family is ever going to come. He is seventy-five years of age; his wife, sixty-five; and they have no children. He is eighty-five years of age; she, seventy-five; and they have no children. At eighty-five, he decides he ought to help God out— or Sarah does—and so he takes a concubine, but God says, "No, I'm going to give you your family through Sarah." Finally, when he reaches one hundred years of age, his ninety-year-old wife delivers a child.

God has a family for Abraham even better than the one he has left behind. He wants to put us in a supernatural family, and he wants to give us a family of great joy. When the child is born, God tells Abraham to give him the name *Isaac*, which means "he laughs." This child is a child of pure joy to God and to Abraham and Sarah. God also gives Abraham a people. He tells Abraham that his descendants will be more than the stars (Gen 15:5). The people of Israel are Abraham's descendants. God gives Abraham his own new people—what a people it has been! Out of all the peoples of the earth, that people has spread more blessing across the world than all the other peoples of the world put together. God will never take anything away but that he gives you something infinitely better.

Finally, God gives Abraham and Sarah a country, he gives them Canaan, and even more, he provides them with an eternal kingdom, that kingdom which is to come when every knee bows and every tongue confesses that Jesus Christ is Lord to the glory of God the Father. That eternal, unshakeable Kingdom is Abraham's inheritance as well as the inheritance of all believers. Scripture's record of Abraham is beautiful to me because it brings us to the essence of what really matters. Abraham is given all those things, but the great thing is that Abraham got God.

God has given Elsie and me five children, and God's given us sixteen grandchildren. God has given us a rather interesting life, a very fascinating calling. I have had experiences nobody else in the world has had. I've been president of Asbury College. I have had the privilege of serving Christ in many places. But do you know the best thing of all? I have had Elsie, and as I have had her and walked with her, all other things have come from that relationship.

All Elsie and I had to do was live and love each other, and we got Beth. The next thing we knew we had Denny. All we had to do was live and love each other and the next thing we knew, we had Katy. All we had to do was live and love each other, and one day the doctor said to me, "I hope you have plenty of bedroom space in your house."

And I said, "What do you mean?"

"Well," he said, "You've got two little girls in there."

And I said, "You're lying!"

"Go see your brand-new twins." I walked into the delivery room, and there were these two baby girls, wiggling together like little earthworms. I looked down and thought, "Mine?" I looked at Elsie, and she said, "How many?"

"Two."

"Are you sure? Are they all right?"

"They look okay to me," I said without knowing what I was talking about. Elsie looked up and said to me with joy on her face, "Isn't that just like the Lord? You ask for one and you get two!"

All of that came just by living with somebody else and loving her and her loving me. There is no telling what will happen if you live with Christ and love him. There will be eternal fruit; it will start a lineage that will run for eternity.

God desires Abraham to live with him, follow him, and trust him, and he promises that good fruit will come from it. That is the word he wants to say to you: if you will keep your relationship to Christ the central reality of your life and the most important thing in your life, your life will cast a shadow like that.

Now let me make three or four comments about the God you get to follow, the One who travels with you. This God is the Lord of all circumstances. He has been Lord in the past, but I want you to know he is the Lord of the future just as much as he is of the past. With God, there is no future. He is in the future as much as he is in the past. One year, I was preparing to preach on the Ascension, and it was one of those moments that blew my mind and I have never gotten over it. I found myself asking: "What is so important about the Ascension; why did the Son go back to the Father? I thought, "How far did he go, and how long did it take him?" And then I laughed and I thought, "That's funny, *how far* is a space question, and *how long* is a time question, and space and time are not a part of eternity." He lives in a world that transcends space and time, so I realized that Jesus did not go anywhere. You cannot say *where* about God; *where* is a space word. And you cannot say *when* about God, because he is eternal. You cannot put him in the past. He is in your future as much as he is in your past or your present, and he is Lord. He controls everything.

One of the fun things about getting old is a long memory, and I can remember some of the times when God said to me, "I want you to pack your bags and move." I was thirty-eight. Elsie and I had five kids and God said, "I want you to pack your bags and go to graduate school."

I said, "There's no way. I don't have any money."

"That's my business." He provided in such amazing ways. I could regale you with story after story. He does not do miracles every day, but he does them when they have to be done, even though his normal mode of operating is through the routine nature of life. He is Lord, and he can take care of you, and it is neither his business nor his way to let you get in a box out of which he cannot get you. When you start your day, you can say, "Our Father, my Father," and he is capable of taking care of you no matter what comes. I want to say that as strongly as I know how. That is the reason he can ask you to stick your neck out for him. He will not let you down; he will take care of you.

Our God will also put his followers in big business. Americans do not have anything to live for beyond ourselves. We are living in a very futile, empty-hearted age. Human persons, made in the image of God, were not created to be satisfied simply with material goods.

God said to Abraham, "If you will follow me, we will save the world." Abraham knew God was in big business, and he wanted to be a part of God's business. This is the only explanation I can find for Abraham's faithfulness across the years.

I do not think Abraham knew how big a business God had involved him in, but he knew God planned to bless the world, and understanding that was enough for Abraham. I remember hearing Henry Clay Morrison preach when I was a student at Asbury College. I love the fact that Morrison always believed he was in the greatest business in the world because he was preaching the gospel. He would not have traded places with anyone in the world, because he could share the good news of Jesus with the world. He knew that if you will walk with Christ, he will put you in big business. The world may not recognize it, but you will know its reality deep in your heart, and there will be a contentment inside you, because you are living for eternal things.

This God of Abraham always goes before you. He never asks you to go where he has not already been, and he will never ask you to do anything that he has not already done. His mode of relating to us is exactly opposite the world's way. He does not operate as a boss who tells his subordinates what to do. He has entered our world, assumed our pain, and borne it with us and for us. You will never find any place where he is not ahead of you to lead you, to guide you, to protect you, to care for you, to be there with you. He will never ask you to do anything that he is not willing to do.

The best example is in Genesis 22 when God asks Abraham to give up his son. "Take your son, your only son, whom you love—Isaac—and go to the region of Moriah. Sacrifice him there as a burnt offering on a mountain I will show you" (Gen 22:2). The next verse says that early the next morning Abraham "got up and loaded his donkey." I cannot imagine how much he suffered through that night, but when the daylight came, he was headed for Mount Moriah to obey the One with whom he walked. As they were going up the mountain,

Isaac turned and said, "Father? . . . The fire and wood are here . . . but where is the lamb for the burnt offering?" (Gen 22:7).

Abraham said, "God himself will provide the lamb." Then Abraham laid his only son on that altar, bound him, and raised the knife to put it in Isaac's breast; there was total obedience in Abraham.

God intervened. He did not want Isaac; he just wanted to know that Abraham had placed God ahead of his only beloved son, that Abraham was still living detached from all else and attached to God and to God alone. God's salvation depended on Abraham's obedience, and as soon as he knew Abraham's heart, he stepped in to save Isaac. Henry Clay Morrison used to describe this scene in a powerful way. He would say:

I thought I heard a conversation on Mount Moriah. It wasn't between Abraham and Isaac, it was between the first Person of the Trinity and the second Person of the Trinity. The second Person of the Blessed Trinity said to the first of the Blessed Trinity, "Father, this is not the last time we're coming to this mountaintop, is it?"

And the Father said to the eternal Son, "No, Son, this is not the last time we're coming to this mountaintop. It will be about two thousand years and we'll be back here."

"Father, when we come back the next time, it won't be one of them on this altar, will it?"

The eternal Father replied, "No, Son, when we come back the next time, it won't be one of them on this altar; it will be one of us."

"It will be me, won't it?"

And the Father said, "Son, yes, it will be you."

The eternal Son looked into the face of the eternal Father and he said, "Father, when we come back the next time, and it's me on that altar, and the knife's raised or the spear is raised, and they're ready to push it in, are you going to say, 'Don't touch the lad'?"

"No, Son. We never ask them to do in symbol what we are not willing to do in reality."[1]

The power and poignancy of that scene has never left me. This is the reason people have been willing to follow Christ to the death. Unlike any other god, God has never asked anything out of you or me that he has not done before us. He asks no surrender of us that he has not already given. The reality is that Christ's sacrifice took place in the heart of eternity, slain from before the foundations of the world in the heart of God. That is the kind of care he has for us. He is not the One who is going to tell us how to do it; he is the One who is going to do it for us. He will never ask you to pay a price he has not already paid.

The last the thing I want to say about our God is that he is the One who keeps every promise he ever makes. He told Abraham he was going to have a son, and he did. Let me give one more of Henry Clay Morrison's illustrations.

> When God said to Abraham that he was going to have a son, Abraham said, "It's obvious you aren't from around here."
>
> God said, "Why is that?"
>
> Abraham said, "Because if you were from around here, you'd know my wife's sixty-five and I'm seventy-five."
>
> God responded, "I'm the eternal One, and years don't make any difference with me. You're going to have a son."

"Now the astounding thing is," Morrison would say, "Abraham believed him."

> The next morning, bright and early, he went downtown to the local furniture store and said to the Jewish storekeeper, "I want the best baby buggy in the house." The owner looked at Abe and said, "What are you going to do with a baby buggy? You're seventy-five years old. Is one of your handmaids going to have a child?"

---

1 Morrison's stories in this chapter are retold in Kinlaw's words based on his memories of Morrison's sermons.

"No," he said, "Listen to me. This is going to be hard on you, but Miss Sarah's going to have a baby."

And the owner said, "Abe, maybe I'd better tell you about the facts of life." And Abe said, "Let me tell you about the facts of God; Miss Sarah is going to have a baby."

Every woman down Abe's street got a crick in her neck as she watched that white-haired old man push that empty baby buggy down the street and watched as he pulled it up over the steps of the porch, and onto the porch, and into the living room, and then parked it beside the fireplace where it sat for the next twenty-five years as a conversational piece.

And every person that came in said, "Abe, why the baby buggy?"

And Abe said, "Do you see these hills? One of these days they are all going to belong to my descendants because God has promised, and that baby buggy is my response to his word to me."

I have remembered that story all my life. That promise of God was fulfilled.

You have a future, but the future is not in you; it is in him. Finding our future is keeping our personal relationship with Christ clean and clear on a day-by-day, hour-by-hour basis. Our attachment to him means that, compared to that attachment, every other relationship in your human experience is a detachment. Simply put, he comes first. And if you make him Lord and leave all to follow him, the rest of us are going to spend eternity listening to the stories you will tell about the outworking of his plan in your life. That is something worth looking forward to!

7
The Mind of Christ

PHILIPPIANS 2

Philippians 2 encapsulated for Papa what a holy heart actually looked like in the hard realities of daily life and personal interactions. He preached this sermon many times, and it always produced a deep conviction of sin and joy in the freedom of full salvation that is available to believers. As I reflected on this sermon recently, I realized that it really was the witness of Papa's life until the very end.

Papa lived with us from his eighty-ninth year until his ninety-fourth year, and during that time he suffered from congestive heart failure. This meant that Papa would have periods of severe weakness, shortness of breath, and serious physical decline. The possibility of death became a reality that my family lived with while Papa shared our home.

As Papa's health declined, we watched Papa as he embraced the Father's will for him. We watched him live out in very practical ways the mind of Christ. After a life of constant motion and activity, of travel and public ministry, Papa was confined to one house and then eventually to one room. We watched as Papa received what his Father gave and received it with joy. He would talk about "my little corner," and, in that corner, he found real happiness in reading and study, in the loved ones who came to visit, and in reading and listening to Scripture. The last year of Papa's life, there were days when he could not read. His hands were not steady enough to hold a book; his eyesight could not read the words; and he wearied with the labor of study. Yet we watched as Papa received each new limitation with surrender and grace. He became more interested in what we had learned and in listening to the experiences and knowledge of family members. He spent more time in intercession and in private worship. Some mornings, I would go in to help him get up, and his eyes would be full of tears because of the love of Christ. He would lie in bed and worship, and, as a family, we received the grace and mercy that worship brought with it.

At the end of life, one's tendency is to be self-absorbed. Fear of the unknown is real, and physical strength is at its lowest ebb. Even trust requires some strength. Some mornings, Papa would say dejectedly to me, "Cricket, I am lost in myself," and then I would watch him lift his face to look at me with love and interest and say, "But how are you?" At that moment, the turn would come, as Papa let the Holy Spirit love through him. As visitors came to see him, Papa chose love and witness. To each one, he would give his witness of Christ and love them in Jesus' name. He encouraged them, prayed for them, and invited them into his own experience of worship. He received the Father's love even when he did not feel it, and he ministered the Father's love to everyone who had the privilege of walking into his room.

This love was particularly obvious to my teenagers. A seventeen-year-old, a fifteen-year-old, and a thirteen-year-old felt themselves to be the delights of his heart. Whenever they would walk in, he would light up and love would pour out of him and into their hearts. To them, Papa's love represented Jesus' love: it was always other-oriented, it was always consistent, and it was always real. This sermon explains how the mind of Christ in God's people creates an atmosphere in which divine love can reign, and in this love people grow and flourish.

So if there is any encouragement in Christ, any comfort from love, any participation in the Spirit, any affection and sympathy, complete my joy by being of the same mind,

having the same love, being in full accord and of one mind. Do nothing from selfish ambition or conceit, but in humility count others more significant than yourselves. Let each of you look not only to his own interests, but also to the interests of others. Have this mind among yourselves, which is yours in Christ Jesus.[1] Have this mind among yourselves, which is yours in Christ Jesus, who, though he was in the form of God, did not count equality with God a thing to be grasped, but emptied himself, by taking the form of a servant, being born in the likeness of men. And being found in human form, he humbled himself by becoming obedient to the point of death, even death on a cross. Therefore God has highly exalted him and bestowed on him the name that is above every name, so that at the name of Jesus every knee should bow, in heaven and on earth and under the earth, and every tongue confess that Jesus Christ is Lord, to the glory of God the Father.

Therefore, my beloved, as you have always obeyed, so now, not only as in my presence but much more in my absence, work out your own salvation with fear and trembling, for it is God who works in you, both to will and to work for his good pleasure.

Do all things without grumbling or disputing, that you may be blameless and innocent, children of God without blemish in the midst of a crooked and twisted generation, among whom you shine as lights in the world, holding fast to the word of life, so that in the day of Christ I may be proud that I did not run in vain or labor in vain. Even if I am to be poured out as a drink offering upon the sacrificial offering of your faith, I am glad and rejoice with you all. Likewise you also should be glad and rejoice with me.

I hope in the Lord Jesus to send Timothy to you soon, so that I too may be cheered by news of you. For I have no one like him, who will be genuinely concerned for your welfare. For they all seek their own interests, not those of Jesus Christ. But you know Timothy's proven worth, how as a son with a father he has served with me in the gospel. I hope therefore to send him just as soon as I see how it will go with me, and I trust in the Lord that shortly I myself will come also. (Philippians 2:1–24 ESV)

---

1 Some texts say, "your attitude should be the same as that of Jesus Christ" or more traditionally, "let this mind be in you which was also in Christ Jesus." A literal translation would be "to be minded the way Christ Jesus is minded."

One of the things that I have noticed about my study of Scripture across the years is that I have found that there are certain passages that come alive for me and become precious to me. Over a period of time, I learned that as I would re-read Scripture and find myself moving toward those special passages, my mind would run over the stuff that was in front of me in anticipation of what was coming in the same way you might forget about the foothills when you see the mountains in the distance. As the years passed, I began to find that some of what I thought were foothills were actually lovely mountains in themselves.

When I was in the pastorate, I decided to preach a series of sermons on great texts before great texts. Then I decided to preach a second series on great texts after great texts. John 3:15 is a great text, and so is John 3:17—and Galatians 2:19 and Galatians 2:21. Because of my weakness for rushing through parts of Scripture, the book of Philippians never quite opened up to me. When I would get through the early part of it, I knew what was coming in Philippians 2:5–11, which is this incredible passage on the incarnation that describes Christ emptying himself and becoming one of us. I didn't pay careful attention to what Paul said before that.

Then one day as I was working my way through it, it dawned on me that Paul didn't write Philippians in order to give us Philippians 2:5–11, because that hymn to Christ is in a sense the illustration, not the sermon. On occasion, I have had people come to me after I have preached and ask me to repeat an interesting illustration, and I knew that they had missed the main point and only remembered the illustration. I realized that what goes before and after that illustration in Philippians 2 is where I find out what it means for me to have the mind of Christ, while in verses 5–11 I find out what it meant for Christ to have the mind of Christ. Those are two different things.

The Philippian letter is a very tender letter, written by Paul to the church that he probably loved the most of any of the churches that he ever served. Remember the story in Acts when Paul was turning to go into Asia and the Spirit checked him and instructed him to go west?

We have received the gospel in the West because of the Spirit's check on Paul. When God stopped him from going into Bithynia, they went to Troas, and Paul had a vision. In that vision, there was a man from Macedonia who stood and pled with him to come over and help. So, Paul turned his steps west and came into Macedonia and eventually to Philippi. When he got to Philippi, he looked around for someone with whom to worship, and he found a group of women—a ladies' prayer meeting. They met down on the riverbank, and their leader was named Lydia. As he began to preach Christ to those ladies, they knew enough to know that what they were hearing was the fulfillment of the Old Testament, which they believed. Lydia said, "Will you baptize me and my house?" Paul baptized them, and she opened her home for a church in Philippi.

When the temple authorities heard of the new believers, there was a riot, and Paul and Silas ended up in jail. They were mercilessly flogged and put into stocks. In the middle of the night, an angel came and an earthquake came, and a Philippian jailer was converted with his entire household. Then before it was over with, the authorities were pleading with them to leave the city. Paul's connection with this little fledgling church was deep and real.

Many years later, Paul was in prison again, except this time he was in prison in Rome. He was in chains and thinking about when this had happened to him before. He had very tender memories about the Christians in Philippi who had loved him and over the years since had regularly been his supporters, sending contributions to him to help him. The reader senses the tenderness in the letter. Paul says, "I thank my God in all my remembrance of you, always in every prayer of mine for you all making my prayer with joy, because of your partnership" (Phil 1:3 ESV). Then he goes on to rejoice at the privilege of being in chains in a Roman prison.

Then Paul turns to the mind of Christ. Paul gives us four characteristics of the person who has the mind of Christ; two of them are given before the hymn and two of them are given afterwards. The first two are: "Do nothing from selfish ambition or conceit" (Phil 2:3

ESV). The last two are: "Do all things without grumbling or disputing" (Phil 2:14 ESV). Now, I looked at the first characteristic of the mind of Christ, "Do nothing from selfish ambition," and I immediately felt relief. When you are as old as I am, you don't worry so much about ambition. Ambition seems to be something for the young and upward moving. So, I thought, "Good, I am clean on that one." Unfortunately, I picked up a Greek New Testament and read it, and the word used there for *selfish ambition* has nothing to do with ambition. Instead it is a word that deals with self-interest. It is a very interesting word. Originally, it had no negative connotation about it; it had to do with a laborer working for wages, which is very legitimate. Then in Greek literature, it developed the connotation of getting more interested in the wages than you were in the work: a workman would do work in order to get something in return. Then the word came to stand for a bribe, and then it became a word used for prostitution, a harlot who wants to seduce a man for what she can get. Slowly, it developed the connotation of self-interest, of "what can I get out of this?"

Age does not have anything to do with self-interest. You can be as old as Methuselah and still be selfish. And that's what we are talking about in this passage, not just ambition in people on the rise. Let me put it this way so that we can apply it to our own lives: do I look at a situation and think, "What is in it for me?" Does that attitude determine my actions or my responses? Age does not deliver you from that attitude. Freedom from that attitude is the first mark of the mind of Christ in this Philippians passage. If you are going to have the mind of Christ, you are not going to look at a new situation—or even an old situation—with the attitude of "what's in it for me?"

That was certainly true of Christ. What motivated him was not what he could get for himself. What motivated him was our need. You will notice that fits the context here because Paul says, "Do nothing from selfish ambition or conceit, but in humility count others more significant than yourselves. Let each of you look not only to his own interests, but also to the interests of others" (Phil 2:3–4 ESV). We are talking about other-orientedness, where the need of the other, not your need, determines how you are going to respond. That is the first mark of the mind of Christ. Understanding that Paul is talking about a life free from self-interest brought it a little closer to home for me.

The second thing this translation says is, "Do nothing from . . . conceit" (Phil 2:3 ESV). Again, my first reaction was indifference; I did not believe that applied to me. When you are as old as I am and you've been beaten down as many times as I have, the conceit is fairly well knocked out of you. But again, I read the Greek text, and the word in Greek for conceit is *kenodoxia*, which is made up of two elements. The *keno* part has to do with emptiness, when there is nothing there. The *doxia* part has to do with appearances or show. Paul was saying, "Don't do anything because of empty appearances." As I wrestled with that, I began to realize what Paul meant: when you have the mind of Christ, you do not ask the question, "How am I going to look?" Your actions are not determined by how you're going to appear to other people. Age does not solve that problem either, because appearances mean as much to old people as they do to young people. Paul did not want the Philippians to be under the tyranny of how they would look if they took a stand for Jesus or if they acted in his name. If you are controlled by the fear of how you will look, you will never stand with Christ. I think that is one of the reasons Peter and the disciples forsook Jesus on Good Friday. Who wants to be identified with a criminal? You can count on it that there will always be a bit of the crucifixion of pride within us in public identification with the ultimate will of God.

Paul knew what it meant to do things for show. Paul had university training. He was a sophisticated Jew. He was a Hebrew of the Hebrews. He was arrogant and proud, and then God came to him and called him to follow the truth by going the way of the lowly Nazarene. Paul knew it would make him an object of contempt and scorn in the minds of all of the people whose favor he had sought. Paul chose Christ, and he did not want anyone to have to live under the tyranny of appearances. I thank God that Jesus was free on that score. How do you think he felt when he was being led naked through the streets and pinned naked on a cross? How he looked did not determine what he did, and because of that, we have redemption in him.

The third characteristic comes after the hymn. Paul says, "Do all things without grumbling or disputing." I didn't have to read the Greek text to understand what that meant because it is very clear. I was surprised that this was a mark of the mind of Christ. What is wrong with grouching a little bit? Certainly, circumstances sometimes warrant it. I dare you to go through the Old Testament and study grumbling. If you do, you will find that God takes it very seriously. Remember when the Israelites found themselves in the wilderness, and there was nothing to eat except manna and quail? They grumbled because they had left behind good food in Egypt. God took their grumbling personally. There are passages in Exodus and Numbers in which grumbling is a deadly insult to God. God said, "I am leading you into redemption. You are exactly where I want you and I'm doing with you exactly what I want to do to get you to where you are supposed to be, and you're sitting around grumbling and complaining about it." As a result, not one of the complaining generation got into the Promised Land. Grumbling will keep you out of the blessing of God.

Why do we complain? I've noticed about myself that I never complain when I am getting better than I know I deserve. As long as I am getting better than I deserve, I never complain. The problem arises when I think I deserve better than what I am given. Then I get unhappy and begin to grumble, "I deserve better than that." Notice the pronoun. Notice these first three—what's in it for *me*, how will *I* look, *I* deserve better than that; implicit in all three is that "me first" mentality.

The one thing you never found on the lips of Jesus was grumbling or complaining. In fact, we are told for the joy that was set before him, he endured the cross. It was not a delight to him, but he endured it for the joy that was set before him, which was our salvation. He endured the cross and despised the shame.

The fourth characteristic of the mind of Christ is: "Do all things without . . . disputing." The Greek word for *dispute* is an interesting word from which we get the word *dialogue*. It has to do with reasoning. I know that God is not opposed to our reasoning because he put a brain in our heads and gave us the gift of reason. I think that this word probably had no negative connotations originally, just like *kenodoxai*. I think it used to describe when a person encounters a new situation or a problem and uses reason to think through it and try to solve that problem in the most intelligent way. However, over a period of time, the word began to be used with a different connotation. It meant a person saw a certain situation and reacted in a way to protect his reputation. The truth is not the central thing, but appearances.

One of the translations uses the word *arguing*. Let me tell you the way it comes home to me. Have you ever noticed how you can have a discussion with somebody where you want the other person to go along with you and the other person wants your approval, so the person will say, "Why yes, but . . . ."? When the *yes* is said, you have hope, and then the guy says *but*, and you know there is resistance. I think that's exactly what Paul is talking about in Philippians. God says, "Kinlaw, here's my will for you." And I say, "Yes, Lord—but." There rises a minority vote inside me that says, "Let's see if there is a way to get out of this one." Jesus never said to his Father, "Yes, Father—but." Christ wholeheartedly embraced the will of the Father. He endured the cross, despising the shame.

With all four characteristics, I found myself saying, "Is it possible for anybody to be like that—to look at a situation without letting self-interest control, without letting 'What is in it for me?' or 'How do I look?' or 'I deserve better than this!' or 'Yes, Lord—but' to determine one's course of action?" The reality is that I am a self, and therefore to any situation that develops, I respond as a self because there isn't any other way for me to respond. These questions are going to arise, but how do we respond? I thought about how Jesus faced these temptations to put himself first. With that in mind, I tried to look back and see how Jesus lived in our circumstances, and I noticed that he had some problems. I read the passage in John 12:20–27 where the Greeks came and wanted to see Jesus. Jesus knew that if the Gentile world was to hear the gospel there was no way except the cross. Jesus lifted up his voice and said, "Now is my soul troubled. And what shall I say? 'Father, save me from this hour?'" As I read the passage, I could feel Jesus recoiling from the cross. He says, "Father, for this purpose came I to this hour." He looked at the pain that awaited him because he was a human being, and he recoiled from it, but he did not let his feelings determine his action. The cross was why he came, and though he did not want it and everything within him cried out against it, he chose to embrace the cross. "But for this purpose [the cross] I have come to this hour" (Jn 12:27 ESV).

I am grateful for the stories we have of Thursday night and Gethsemane. Jesus was a few hours from the cross, and he went to talk to his Father about it. He came back to his disciples, but he had not settled the issue with his Father, so he went back and prayed again. When he came back after the second time, he still did not have grace for what awaited him, and so he went back and prayed the third time. When he prayed the third time, it was settled. When he came back, he was ready to face those who came to arrest him. I appreciate that the eternal Son of God did not want the Father's will for him, and he found within himself emotions that recoiled against it. But it was not the feelings that determined what he did. He faced all the trauma of it, and then, in spite of its horror, he put his arms around it and said, "Father, not my will but yours be done." There is no mechanical, automaton kind of obedience here. If obedience cost Jesus the painful surrender of his own rights and will, I believe our own Gethsemane moments will be painful as well. As we learn surrender in these moments, we will have the joy of participating with Christ Jesus in the suffering and in the glory of the cross.

Paul did not want Gethsemane moments to stop Christians from doing the will of the Father: "Let this mind be in you which was in Christ Jesus." The person with the mind of Christ can look at the will of the Father, no matter how painful it is, and say, "Not my will but yours be done." That is the way Jesus responded to his Father's will.

In 1 Corinthians 10:24, Paul gives one of the strongest words in the New Testament: "No one should seek their own good, but the good of others." What fascinates me about Paul's comment is that there is no equivocation and there is no condition attached to it. The Greek just simply, bluntly says, "Nobody should seek the things of himself." The word *good* is not in there; it just says, "Nobody should seek the things of himself, but every person should seek the things of another." The real question for me was whether anyone could actually live that way. I had read the literature where Paul calls himself the chief of sinners, and that encouraged me because I figured there was substantial hope for me if he was the chief of sinners. Then I noticed 1 Corinthians 10:31–33: "So whether you eat or drink or whatever you do, do it all for the glory of God. . . . even as I try to please everyone in every way. For I am not seeking my own good but the good of many, so that they may be saved." The law of Paul's life was not self-interest; it was the well-being of somebody else that determined who Paul was. Then he said to the Corinthians, "Follow my example" (1 Cor 11:1). This way of life was possible for Paul, and it is possible for us.

The very thought of what Paul is proposing is difficult for Christians to accept, but he illustrates it in Philippians 2:4: "Each of you look not only to his own interests, but also to the interests of others" (ESV). I was comfortable with this passage until I looked at the Greek, but when I looked at the Greek, I could not find the word *only* in there. Isn't it interesting how different the presence of that word *only* makes? Because if the word *only* is in that verse, I have every right to look to some of my own interest. If the word *only* is not in the text, it means something entirely different. The word that is normally translated *only* is the Greek word *kai*, and *kai* can be translated both *also* and *even*. I thought "Kinlaw, you don't know enough about this grammar to make any conclusions," so I went to our classical Greek professor at Asbury College, and I said, "I want you to translate a verse for me." I pulled that verse out just by itself and made him translate it, and he translated it without the *only* in there. Then I went to Dr.

Robert Mulholland, the provost at Asbury Theological Seminary, who had a Harvard PhD in New Testament.

I said, "Bob, would you translate this verse for me out of the Greek?" He translated it without the word *only*. And so I said to him, "Bob, that's not the way the passage is translated." So, I showed him the English. He went to his shelf and began pulling down his grammars and his lexicons. He came back to me and said, "You know, Dennis, I don't believe it belongs in there." I raised the same issue with another friend of mine who was a better New Testament scholar than I. He was one of the translators of the NIV. He got very upset with me. It is hard for anyone to translate the Bible because the standard is so high.

Paul said this life was possible. Paul did not live under the tyranny of "what's in it for me?" or "how will I look?" or "I deserve better than this" or "yes, Lord—but." Paul further illustrates this life: "I hope in the Lord Jesus to send Timothy to you soon, that I also may be cheered when I receive news about you. I have no one else like him, who will show genuine concern for your welfare. For everyone looks out for their own interests, not those of Jesus Christ. But you know that Timothy has proved himself, because as a son with his father he has served with me in the work of the gospel" (Phil 2:19–22). I thought, for heaven's sake, Paul knew how to live this way and so did Timothy. The law of Timothy's life was not self-interest but the will of Christ and the wellbeing of others.

Immediately, I began to wonder how they got to that place. Timothy did not seem nearly as exceptional as Paul, and then I read verses 12 and 13: "Therefore, my dear friends, as you have always obeyed—not only in my presence, but now much more in my absence—continue to work out your salvation with fear and trembling, for it is God who works in you to will and to act in order to fulfill his good purpose." I began to comprehend that Paul did not live there because he was exceptional: he lived there because of grace. If Timothy got there, I do not think I have an excuse for not getting there. Because if the grace of God could bring Timothy to where he was not under the tyranny of self-interest, then by that same grace we can put our arms around life and accept it as God gives it to us, and it will be the grace of God that enables us to do it. What a difference it would make if a person would let God liberate him or her to live that way. That is the way Jesus lived, and when he lived that way, the world had an opportunity for redemption.

Helen Roseveare came and spoke at Asbury College, and I will never forget her testimony. She was a Cambridge graduate with a medical degree, and she spent her life in Africa serving as a doctor. Then one day there was an uprising, and the rebels captured her and many other women. They brutalized her and raped her multiple times. As the horror of that descended on her, she said it was like the blackness of hell. And then she said, "I heard a voice, and the voice said, 'Thank you, Helen, for letting me use your body. It is not you that they rape; it is me.'" Her healing came as she held on to that word from her Lord Jesus, and she came through victoriously. She was home on furlough trying to put her life back together before going back and she was at one of the universities. She was speaking and noticed in that university crowd two girls, one of whom was far too young to be a university student. They sat on the end of a row of seats. When she finished her lecture, the audience left and she went to get her briefcase, and when she came back she noticed the two girls hadn't moved. She started toward them, and the older girl came to her and said, "A few weeks ago, my sister who is here was raped, and from that moment to this, she has never uttered a word. She is in total shock. Could you talk to her?" Helen Roseveare said, "I turned and all of the horror of my own experience flooded back over me, and then even more powerfully the memory of the presence of Jesus." And as she started for the girl, the girl bounded out of her seat and ran into Helen's arms. They wept together for the better part of an hour. Helen never said, "I deserve better than this." She allowed Jesus to meet her in the middle of her pain, and then she allowed him to transform it to something that could be a blessing to another.

If Christ is sovereign, and if he is Lord and I give him my life, is there anything that comes to me that I can separate from his choice?

And if he's the one giving it, don't tell me he doesn't give it with redemptive purposes in mind.

I have come to believe that there is grace that can enable a person to live. Nobody's going to get to the place where they never ask the question, "What is in it for me?" but we do not have to be controlled by the answer. We can say by his grace, "Father, if it's your will, I can put my arms around it and embrace it."

"How will I look?" I don't like to look like a fool any more than anybody else. We might recoil from what seems like shame, but by his grace we can say, "Father, if it's your will, I can put my arms around it, because I won't have to go through it alone."

"I deserve better than this." No, no, no. If we are following him, how can that issue ever be raised? But the hardest one is, how can we get to the place where the *but* doesn't follow the *yes*? That is why I believe in the message of heart holiness. I believe Jesus can take the resistance, the recalcitrance, out of our hearts and our minds. We can look at all the negatives life brings and still say, "That's all right, Lord. I consciously, deliberately choose it because I know it's from you." He delivers you from "Yes Lord—but."

More than anything else, our world needs Christians to have the mind of Christ. If we don't, when we get in the middle of life's most difficult places, our witness will not be the same as his. There will be two voices instead of one, and one will be the voice of self-interest. If we let him bring us to the place where his will has become ours and his mind controls ours, then we will find that any witness we have is identical with his, and the world can see who Jesus Christ really is.

We are never ahead of him in our witness. He is always first in every person's life, drawing each one to himself. God wants to set us free from the tyranny of our own self-way and self-interest. He wants us to begin to entertain the thought that it might be possible for us to put our arms around his will and for us to embrace it, no matter what it is. If we get to the point where we believe that it's possible, he is going to do something in our hearts to enable us to embrace it. If we ask him sincerely, he can do it. What we will find is that when we have asked him and he has helped us to embrace what we do not want, we will find that he can take us victoriously through it, and out of it will come something redemptive.

8

Worship at the Heart of Life

PSALM 8

Papa became Asbury College's seventh president in 1968. God led him to accept the College's invitation even though it meant putting aside his career as a Biblical Studies professor at Asbury Theological Seminary. Although leaving his Hebrew classes was a source of grief to him, one of the things that quickly captured his mind and imagination was the doctrine of creation that underlies a Christian liberal arts program. He became enamored with the world that God created and learned everything about it that he could. He would interview each prospective faculty member not only to see if they would be a good fit for the position but also to learn about their area of expertise. He became a passionate learner of not just ancient languages but of every discipline. He believed that God was the center of education and that humans were given a command to learn and cultivate our world. Worship of the triune God was the pivot around which everything turned, creating a culture of free and intensive study.

Psalm 8 and Genesis 1–2 became the foundational scriptures for his way of thinking about Christian liberal arts studies. Christians should learn all they can to be ready for the responsibilities God will give them. Fear of new scientific knowledge or even of new technology was unknown to him. Learning was an adventure with Christ until he died at age ninety-four, and all knowledge could be used to win the world to the One he loved so much.

Ultimately, even more than studying about God's world, Papa believed that knowing the triune God through Jesus Christ was the key to life itself. He would talk about interpersonal relationships, how one person changes when another person walks in the room. We watched this as Papa became confined to his bedroom. When someone would come to visit him, his face would light up, his body would lean forward, and his whole demeanor would change. He anticipated the joy that would come from the interaction, and it filled him with delight and energy. In the same way, Papa believed that when Christ walked into a person's life, that entire life would change; worship and anticipation were the evidences of Christ's presence in a person's life. Knowing Christ was better than knowing about him or knowing about his world. The greatest source of wonder in Papa's life was the intimacy that was available to the follower of Jesus. Knowing the Father, through the Son and the Spirit, was the greatest joy and the greatest adventure he could imagine. His prayer was that everyone would know the joy and the excitement that comes from knowing Christ Jesus.

This sermon was preached at Asbury College at the beginning of a new quarter. Papa wanted to make clear for Asbury students and faculty that Jesus Christ was central to all aspects of education and that worship was the heart of all learning. Knowing Christ was the key to knowing everything about creation.

Lord, our Lord, *how majestic is your name in all the earth!*

You have set your glory in the heavens. Through the praise of children and infants you have established a stronghold against your enemies, to silence the foe and the avenger. When I consider your heavens, the work of your fingers, the moon and the stars, which you have set in place,

what is mankind that you are mindful of them, human beings
that you care for them?

You have made them a little lower than the angels and
crowned them with glory and honor. You made them rulers
over the works of your hands; you put everything under
their feet: all flocks and herds, and the animals of the wild,
the birds in the sky, and the fish in the sea, all that swim the
paths of the seas.

Lord, *our Lord, how majestic is your name in all the*
earth! (Psalm 8)

New beginnings are a time of new opportunities, and they represent new privileges. It is appropriate that we begin each new season or chapter in our lives or education by worshipping God, the One who has given these new opportunities to us. Not everybody understands why we open a new academic year with worship. There are thousands of educational institutions in this country today, and hundreds of thousands of students in those universities, where there is no opportunity for a chapel service like this to take place.

As Christians, we have a different understanding of time. We do not believe that hours and days are due to us as our right, nor do we believe that they are of our own making, nor that they are simply the result of meaningless chance operative in our universe. We believe that time is a gift, a personal gift from a personal giver. We believe that the time we have here together is a gift from the hand of our loving God, and so we stop today and thank him for the gift of this new beginning.

Many in the educational or secular world feel that it is quite inappropriate to introduce God into the study of secular material. They insist on a radical separation between school and God, learning and religion. It is as if we have forgotten, as a people, from whence we have come. We need to remember that even the most secular university in this country owes the very concept that gave it its existence to the Church. The Bible and the Church are the womb out of which the Western university was born. Our universities, whether secular or religious, came from those cathedral and monastery schools of the Middle Ages. In fact, all the original colleges in the United States were committedly Christian.

Two major factors led to the rise of what we speak of as the college or university in Western culture. One of those factors is an incredibly simple concept, and, if we think about it, it should be an obvious one: all truth is one. It forms a tapestry, and, if we could see it correctly, we would see a unity about knowledge no matter at which end we started. If we ever see it all, we will know that it is all interrelated, all part of a single whole. Because Christians believe in a common origin for all things, we believe that whether one studies biology or whether one studies history, both the professor and the student have their origin in the Creator. The secular university may not teach the doctrine of creation, but the university itself exists because somebody once believed in the Creator and somebody once believed the creation accounts that we find in Genesis 1 and 2.

The second factor that has contributed to the rise of the college and the university in our culture is found in Genesis 1:28: "God blessed them [Adam and Eve] and said to them, 'Be fruitful and increase in number; fill the earth and subdue it. Rule over the fish in the sea and the birds in the sky and over every living creature that moves on the ground.'" This command to fill the earth, subdue, and rule it is reflected in Psalm 8. Some commentators believe that Psalm 8 is a description, or at least an expression, of worship that arose out of the reading of the first chapter of Genesis. The psalm states that men and women have been made a little lower than God himself and that when God made them—when God made you and me—he made us to rule over the rest of the creation. When we study the vastness of the universe or when we explore the intricacies of modern medicine, it is in direct obedience to the commands found in Genesis 1. Human beings were created to master and to rule, and the way that we come to do that is by knowing that world of which we are a part. Study and gaining knowledge of our world is not a secular pursuit but one that has been commanded by God. What we do at this educational institution, whether it is in chapel, in class, or on the ball field, is all in fulfillment of a divine command.

Genesis 1 contains an important word: humans are told to *subdue* the creation. God may be to many people in educational institutions an illegitimate subject, but as far as scriptural and historical realities are concerned, he is the main player in it all. It is appropriate today that we should acknowledge him and that we should worship him.

We need to do more than acknowledge him; we need to come to *know* him. There is an interesting problem when we talk about knowing God, because we also talk about knowing psychology and mathematics and history. We are to know the creation so we can master it and fulfill the purposes that God has for us. Scripture declares that he wants to make himself available to us personally so that we may know him intimately as a friend, as Lord, and as the One in whom we find our greatest personal fulfillment.

Two types of knowing are possible. Knowing God is a very different kind of knowledge from the kind of knowledge that we find in the areas of our activities in an institution like this. It is so different that often the university or the college can be one of the easiest places in which we lose the knowledge of God. In our gaining knowledge of everything else, we forget God and do not know that we have missed knowing the greatest thing of all or the greatest person of all: God himself.

Even at Christian schools, we can miss knowing Christ. Many students have graduated from Asbury College without any personal knowledge of him. One of the finest scientists that I know is a young man who, several years out of his experience at Asbury College, in a succession of events engineered by God himself, came to know God, and his total life was transformed. He shared with me his attitude about Asbury before he met Christ and afterwards. Before he knew Christ, his attitude was one of hostility toward the Christian environment in which he attended school. After he met Christ, he was open to the message of Jesus shared at Asbury.

This can even be true of theological schools, because when you study in a theological school, you are using basically the same pattern for knowledge and the same kind of approach to knowledge and to truth that is used in other educational institutions. I have found that there are many people who are graduates of theological institutions across the United States who have never come to know personally and intimately the God behind the studies of theology. John Wesley came to know Christ when he was thirty-five years of age—after he had finished Oxford and his theological training in his early twenties. More than a decade afterward, he came into a personal relationship with the living God in Jesus Christ.

I think the difference between the two kinds of knowledge can be expressed in two expressions: "to know" and "to know about." A substantial chunk of what you will be doing in a liberal arts college is learning to *know about*. There will be an area of knowledge that you want to master. You will bring it under your scrutiny, give it your time and energy, and discipline yourself to study intensely that particular area of knowledge. Before you finish the course of study, the professor will give you an examination, and the purpose of that examination is to see if you have come to a mastery of that material.

When it comes to the business of *knowing about*, the word "control" epitomizes this type of knowledge. That is the purpose of every examination you will ever have while you are in school. The purpose of this institution is to give you control over material, over skills—to give you mastery in those areas.

In that kind of search for knowledge, the emphasis is, to a certain extent, upon detachment. The role you play is primarily the role of an observer, where you step back and look at that body of knowledge, or look at that bit of information, or look at those skills and try to find a way to master them. You find that the information with which you are dealing is a subject to be known, to be observed, to be controlled, and the purpose of the control is so that we can use that knowledge and we can use it in our position as masters of the creation. This intensity of study and focus takes time, energy, and concentration. This is appropriate for the knowledge of the creation which God has given to us.

When we come to the matter of knowing Christ, we move into a totally different area, style, and methodology, and if we take the method of *knowing about* into our *knowing him*, we will find that we have hit an impenetrable wall. There will be no results that will come to us from it, because we have used the wrong procedure in a different area of research and investigation. If the key word in *knowing about* is *control*, the key word when it comes to *knowing God* is *surrender*.

When we come to God, it is not our business to capture him, or dissect him, or even find out how he operates. It is not our business to observe him and see how he performs and if he does it right. It is not our business to order him to appear on our demand so we can be prepared for whatever test is to come. If we are to know Christ, he is the One who will take the initiative. If he doesn't take the initiative, you will never find him, because it is in his power to know and to be known. He is the One who must give himself to us if we are to know him, and he is the One who must make himself available to us if we would know him. What a radically different context for knowing than that which we find in the typical course that we have. If we use the one method in the other area, we will preclude the very thing that we seek.

Immediately after Thanksgiving, we had a renewal conference here on campus. About one hundred and ten people came from across the country and across the world to gather just to pray together and to spend a few days in seeking to know Christ. One of the persons that I met was a young man who had just completed his doctrinal training in theology. He was very intelligent and listened intently throughout the entire conference. At the end of our time together, he sat down with two people from our group, and he said, "I cannot express to you my appreciation for these two days. I don't really have words adequate to express my gratitude. These two days have given me back my Bible, because graduate school took it away from me."

The subject of theology is God, and the author and subject of Scripture is God. But the methodology used to teach theology and to which this young man subscribed and found himself unknowingly the victim, was that he had to become the master of the Scripture. He said,

"In the last couple days, I have found that I must let it become master of me. The loss of the Scripture for me was unwitting, it happened before I knew it." But he said, "The glorious thing is that in these two days it's been restored and, with that restoration, an access to the God who gave it to me." What a tragedy when we obey the command of God to know his creation and we inadvertently miss him, and what a tragedy when we want to know him, but we substitute knowing about him for the personal knowledge of him.

What are the marks of knowing Jesus instead of knowing about him? Psalm 63 is crucial to help us understand the difference. The amazing thing to me about Psalm 63 is the author of the psalm had never read a single Gospel, did not own a New Testament, and had never celebrated Christmas or Easter. He did not even have the Old Testament. And yet, I want you to notice the intimacy with which he speaks about his relationship to God.

"You, God, are my God . . ." The psalmist claims Yahweh as his own. It is one matter to believe in the existence of God and another thing to know him as your own. The original language could be translated, "O God, you are my God from among all the gods."

". . . earnestly I seek you . . ." The breaking of day will find me seeking you. Every new day, what is our chief business? To know Christ.

"I thirst for you, my whole being longs for you, in a dry and parched land where there is no water." The Hebrew says, "My flesh longs for you in a dry and thirsty land where there is no water."

"I have seen you in the sanctuary and beheld your power and your glory." Isn't it interesting when God is no longer an option in your life any more than bread and water are? Eating and drinking, for most people, are not decisions. It is so much a part of our lives that we instinctively move to meet the need, and we turn without a choice to seek the satisfaction of those needs. This is the language the psalmist uses. He has come to the place where God is not an option; he is as necessary for existence as food and drink, and it takes no more discipline to seek and find God than it does to seek and find food.

"Because your love is better than life . . ." Do you know anything the average person values more than life? Do you know how far we will go to save a life? Everything is in second place to that. We even put the saving of another person's life as primary over our personal needs when the occasion demands. The psalmist says, "Do you know, I have found that the Lord is more valuable than life itself?" Did you know that a person can get to the place where the presence of God in his life is more important than existence? That may have been written a thousand years before Jesus Christ was born. If this man came to know God that intimately without knowing about Christ, how intimately can I know him? If he could say the love of God is better than life with his little knowledge of the love of God, what kind of passion ought to move me who knows so much about the love of God that has been manifested to us in Christ?

". . . my lips will glorify you. I will praise you as long as I live, and in your name I will lift up my hands." Knowledge of God, expressed like this in Scripture, where sin is confessed and the relationship is clean, produces a context of joy and praise. If we ever come to know him, we will find our joy in him, and we will find incredible gratitude and praise for the privilege of knowing him. Certainly, there is joy and pleasure in mastering a body of material, but there is a blessing and delight in knowing God that is not found in any other area of human knowledge.

"I will be fully satisfied as with the richest of foods; with singing lips my mouth will praise you. On my bed, I remember you; I think of you through the watches of the night." It almost sounds as if the psalmist wants to wake up so he can think about his Lord.

"Because you are my help, I sing in the shadow of your wings. I cling to you; your right hand upholds me. . . . the king will rejoice in God." A king is the author of this psalm.

"But the king will rejoice in God; all who swear by God will glory in him, while the mouths of liars will be silenced." He is the God of truth, and when we come to know him, we know the reality that will

ultimately stand, and we are dealing with the One who will outlast all else, because he is God.

As I think about our new beginning and this year, I hope when these next ten weeks are over, you and I will know more than we know today about many things. It is God's world, and he wants us to know every aspect of it. I hope that with all of our knowing, somehow we will get beyond simply *knowing about* God and get to the place where we *know* him. That is why we have chapel as well as classes. That is why we have other religious activities here, as well as our academic interests. We believe it is not enough simply to know the creation, but the greatest of all knowledge is to know the Creator. Those two types of knowledge are not incompatible. The person who worships rightly in chapel will have an openness and a hunger for the knowledge that comes in the classroom.

9
The Marriage Metaphor

JOHN 2:1-11

The fact that Jesus began his public ministry with a wedding intrigued Papa. He began to work on this story to try to understand why the God of the universe would begin his redemptive ministry of the world at a wedding, providing refreshments. This began an intellectual journey for him as he came to understand all of human history in terms of a wedding. As he would say, history began with a wedding in the garden of Eden, and it is going to end with a wedding at the marriage supper of the Lamb. Jesus identified himself as the bridegroom, and John the Baptist identified him as the bridegroom. Papa began to unpack the marital metaphor in Scripture, and it had astounding results in his intellectual life.

Papa believed that we are made for another. We are made for God himself, and the marriage covenant is the best way to understand the intimacy that exists between the Father, the Son, and the Holy Spirit, as well as the intimacy that the Father and the Son desire to have with their creation through the Holy Spirit. The unity in difference, exhibited in marriage, gave an ideal picture of the three in one that is revealed in the Trinity.

For Papa, marriage was a symbol given to the human race of what the divine life is like and what it is like to join in that life. This sermon displays some of the intellectual journey that took place in

Papa's heart and mind in order to formulate his understanding of the marital metaphor in Scripture.

Papa was also interested in the marital metaphor because he and my grandmother, Elsie Blake Kinlaw, shared an uncommon love. Their love for each other flowed naturally out of their love for Christ. My grandmother, Elsie Blake, grew up in Schenectady, New York. She found her way to Asbury College because she was reading a list of colleges in the Almanac, and she thought Asbury had a pretty name. She sent for a catalog, and the day the catalog arrived in the mail, her father had a conversation with a man who told him that God was at work at a little college in Wilmore, Kentucky, called Asbury. He walked into his home and said to my grandmother, "Honey, you are going to go to Asbury College!" He looked down at the table where she was sitting, and there was the Asbury College catalog. In a few months, my grandmother was at Asbury, and in the first few weeks, Henry Clay Morrison preached in chapel, and my grandmother gave her heart to Christ. Not long after that, she was coming down the stairs of her dormitory, and the Spirit said to her heart, "You have given your heart to Christ, wouldn't you like to give him all of your life?" In simple joy, she said, "Yes!" And that "yes" determined the rest of her life. Soon after that entire surrender, she gave her testimony at prayer meeting, and who should be listening but a serious young man by the name of Dennis Kinlaw. The next day found Papa waiting for my grandmother in the college post office. Her witness to Christ drew him to her, and their love story began and grew out of the greater love story of Christ for his creation.

My grandmother's love for Papa and Papa's love for her was second only to their shared love for Christ. Their story became for Papa the best window on what it meant to live in the love of the triune God.

On the third day a wedding took place at Cana in Galilee. Jesus' mother was there, and Jesus and his disciples had also

been invited to the wedding. When the wine was gone, Jesus'
mother said to him, "They have no more wine."

"Woman, why do you involve me?" Jesus replied. "My
hour has not yet come."

His mother said to the servants, "Do whatever he tells
you."

Nearby stood six stone water jars, the kind used by the
Jews for ceremonial washing, each holding from twenty to
thirty gallons.

Jesus said to the servants, "Fill the jars with water"; so
they filled them to the brim.

Then he told them, "Now draw some out and take it to the
master of the banquet."

They did so, and the master of the banquet tasted the
water that had been turned into wine. . . . Then he called the
bridegroom aside and said, "Everyone brings out the choice
wine first and then the cheaper wine after the guest have
had too much to drink; but you have saved the best till now."
(John 2:1–12)

The story of the wedding of Cana has probably affected me as much as any twelve verses in the Scripture. It was late beginning its intellectual and spiritual influence in my life, but its significance has continued to become clearer and more meaningful to me ever since.

I was forty before I ever preached on John 2. Honestly, I did not have the vaguest notion what to do with this crazy start to Jesus' ministry. After all, I am a prohibitionist from North Carolina; what in the world could I say about Jesus making wine at a wedding reception? Even worse than that complication, I could not understand the purpose of this story and could not imagine why Jesus started his ministry with this miracle.

Conquering death and saving the world were the mission of Christ's coming, and he began his ministry for the redemption of the world making refreshments? Jesus came to a social event, and he made wine so a girl and a boy and their families would not be embarrassed. John only recorded seven miracles in his Gospel. He called them signs, every miracle pointing beyond itself to something in the eternal nature of God. It seemed easy for me to understand the sign in the feeding of the five thousand; I could relate that to the Lord's supper.

I could comprehend the blind man receiving his sight because that is what happens when a person finds Christ: he sees clearly for the first time. I could understand Christ's reason for raising Lazarus: Christ conquered death. I understood those signs, but what under the sun could this sign of a wedding mean?

My thinking on this passage of Scripture was triggered one day when I had a British friend come and preach for me. We were starting a church, and I was preaching in a large old house to about ninety people; forty-five would sit in the living room and forty-five in the dining room. One Sunday night, when we went into the house, I looked and noticed twenty-three teenagers who were present from another church. They had heard that there was a church in the area that had an evening service. Because they had never heard of such a thing, their leader decided to bring them. I looked at my visiting preacher and said, "Peter, I don't know what you are going to preach, but you have got twenty-three kids here that may never have heard the gospel clearly."

Our pulpit was a little podium. I will never forget the way he walked up to it, laid his arm on it, sort of rested on it, and said, "The Bible teaches the rightness of short courtships, because my text tonight is John 2:1, 'And the third day, there was a wedding in Cana of Galilee.'" It was a joke, but immediately those twenty-three young people could imagine a boy walking down one side of the street, looking across and seeing a pretty girl, and she looks back and doesn't object, and three days later there is a wedding in Cana of Galilee.

His introduction started my thinking, and I went back to re-read the account of this story to find out what the text really was attempting to communicate. John is very careful to describe the first days of Jesus' ministry. First, he tells of John the Baptist baptizing Jesus by the Jordan River. The temple leadership hear rumors of a man who could be the Christ, and they send a delegation to question him. When asked if he is the Christ, John immediately declares that he is the one coming before him to introduce him to the people of Israel. When John sees Jesus coming to him at the Jordan river, he declares, "Look, the Lamb of God who takes away the sin of the world!" (Jn 1:29). Then Andrew and another man, perhaps John, come to Jesus and say to him, "Where are you staying?" And Jesus invites them to come and see; they go home with him and spend the day with him. Afterwards, Andrew invites Simon, his brother, to meet Jesus. The next day, Jesus sees Philip, and he says to him, "Follow Me," and Philip brings his buddy Nathaniel. So, Jesus picks up four or maybe five of his disciples in those two days. Jesus' team is beginning to come together.

This is the context for the story of the wedding at Cana. Three days later, a wedding occurs, and it is the first story in the public ministry of Jesus. This story tantalized me, because John has a purpose in every incident in the life of Jesus that he chose to tell. Slowly, I began trying to discover what Jesus was up to in this beginning miracle. As I read back through the story, I found a clue to Jesus' purpose in the story of John the Baptist when he was being questioned by the temple authorities in John 3. When they asked John about Jesus stealing his crowds, John said, "He must become greater; I must become less" (Jn 3:30). All preachers love that verse; it is an awfully good text for preaching. I read the context for that verse and was amazed by it. "You yourselves can testify that I said 'I am not the Messiah but am sent ahead of him.' The bride belongs to the bridegroom. The friend who attends the bridegroom waits and listens for him, and is full of joy when he hears the bridegroom's voice. That joy is mine, and it is now complete. He must become greater; I must become less" (Jn 3:28–30). As I read John's words, I thought, "For heaven's sake, is John the Baptist going to explain the redemption of the world in nuptial terms?" That was exactly what he was doing, and I found my mind blown away.

Upon further study, I found that this wedding metaphor is used three times in the synoptic gospels. When the Pharisees questioned Jesus about fasting, his response was in terms of a wedding party: "How can the guests of the bridegroom fast while he is with them? They cannot, so long as they have him with them. But the time will come when the bridegroom will be taken away from them, and on that day they will fast" (Mk 2:19–20). In the early Church, they said that it was as wrong to fast on a feast day as it was to feast on a fast day. Jesus referred to himself as the bridegroom and to his disciples as the guests at his wedding party.

Then suddenly, as I studied, I thought, "Not only John understood the redemptive purposes of God in the incarnation, the cross, the resurrection, and the ascension in nuptial terms: that was the way Jesus looked at it, too." My attention was immediately drawn to Matthew 22. Jesus was in Jerusalem for the last time before the crucifixion, and the temple was ready to kill him, so he told the crowd a story of a king who prepared a wedding feast for his son. He invited all the appropriate guests, but none of the guests wanted to come, so he instructed his servants to go out into the highways and the byways and find anybody willing to come into the wedding party (Matt 22:1–14).

Jesus' philosophy of history and salvation was illustrated in that story. God had chosen Israel so the world could know the gospel, and Israel was invited to be a part of the very marriage of the eternal Son of God, but they rejected their King and his son, and so God opened the door to all the others who would come and receive directly the salvation offered by Jesus. No longer must the world go through the Jews; the good news of Jesus was available to anyone who would believe in him. The story of the redemption of the world, and our inclusion in the kingdom of God, was explained right there in terms of a wedding party.

Jesus' paradigm for salvation was not the courtroom but a wedding. And suddenly, I remembered a wedding was the way human history began. It didn't begin with a church service; it didn't begin with a sacrifice; it didn't begin with a political event; it began with a marriage, and God was the One who orchestrated it. I have always loved the creation story of Adam. I imagine a conversation between God and Adam going something like this:

God said, "Son, how do you like my work?"

"Well, Father," he says, "it is magnificent, but there is nobody here that is like me."

Not a bit surprised, God replied, "I am so glad you caught on, because I wanted you to know that you needed her—that you were incomplete without her."

God took part of Adam and made his companion, and the two of them become one flesh, and a man was instructed to leave father and mother and cling to his wife. All of that was given to us in the creation story, and nothing like it can be found in any other literature of the world.

As I thought about the beginning of creation, I began to think about the end of human history. I realized with a shock that a wedding will be the way human history comes to its completion. Many times, preachers want history to end at the judgment bar, so we can convict people of sin and get them saved from hell, but human history is going to end with a wedding. It is the final chapter. The judgment bar will come, but the end will be the wedding. The last word is going to be nuptial, and Revelation 22 pictures New Jerusalem coming down as a bride adorned for her husband.

There was a wedding in the Garden, and there will be a wedding at the end of history. Which one is the real one? Then it dawned on me that the first was a symbol; what baptism is to salvation, marriage is to your ultimate relationship to Christ. God gave Elsie to me to get me ready for the wedding supper of the Lamb.

One of the surprising things that happened to me as I lived with Elsie was that I was happiest when I could make her happy—even happier than when she made me happy. If she was not pleased, I was unhappy; in fact, the key to my happiness was in her, and the interesting thing is, the key to her happiness was in me. The last year of our fifty-nine years together, Elsie was very sick. I had the responsibility of taking care of her, so I cleared my schedule, and I found there were weeks when the longest trip I would take was to the mailbox out in front of our house.

If you had told me ahead of time what that year would have looked like, I would have dreaded the confinement and isolation, but the shock of my life came when I found it full of joy. I remember thinking to myself, "This is the way it is supposed to be," and the best eleven months of our fifty-nine and a half years were the last eleven months. There was a pure joy in the pain. There was not a thing she could do for me except love me, and there was very little I could do for her except love her. She was my security, and I was her security. I found out in those days that she knew that I loved her, and I knew she loved me. It was the most flattering thing that has ever come to me, to be loved the way she loved me. I have been loved with the kind of love where your concern is for the other and not for yourself.

Once I began to see redemptive history in terms of the nuptial metaphor, I found it all over the Scriptures, and I began a fascinating study. The passage from Exodus 19:4–5 suddenly seemed brand new: "You yourselves have seen what I did to Egypt, and how I carried you on eagles' wings and brought you to myself. Now if you obey me fully and keep my covenant, then out of all nations you will be my treasured possession." He had not brought them into Canaan but to himself, because he wanted them to be his "treasured possession."

The Hebrew expression "treasured possession," *segulah*, occurs only eight times in the Old Testament. It was a jewelers' term for an incredibly valuable piece of jewelry. *Segulah* is something exquisitely beautiful, bringing great delight to the person who owns it. God said to this people whom he had redeemed from slavery, "I brought you to myself, and you are my exquisite treasure." That sounds like marriage language to me.

Hosea thought that Sinai was a marital covenant, and the word out of Sinai was the command to "love the LORD your God with all your heart and with all your soul and with all your strength" (Deut 6:5). In the New Testament, Paul said that love was the fulfillment of the law given at Sinai (Rom 13:10). The fulfillment of Sinai was understood not as obedience but as a perfection of love that would cause one person to lay his or her life down for another. A person can obey a judge and hate him at the same time, but you cannot love God and hate him. If you love him, you are going to want to please him, and you will find your joy is in pleasing him.

When I began to see Scripture in light of this marital metaphor, all my thinking about the Christian life changed drastically. Back in the '60s, I was asked to do a commentary on the Song of Songs. Of course, the reason I got the chance to do the Song of Songs was all the good books had been given away already. I received the assignment of the Song of Songs and Ecclesiastes.

I was forced to shut myself in with the Hebrew text of those two books, and I discovered some amazing truths about God's word. In the Song of Songs, scholars cannot prove that the name of God occurs in it anywhere, and there is nothing in it about religion. It is simply love literature between a man and a woman, and it is in the middle of the Bible. The reason I believe it is in Scripture is the same reason that John chose the wedding at Cana as his first sign. The biblical texts give the reader to understand marital love as a signpost to the triune agape love of God.

In the Song of Songs, there is no reference made to children. The absence of this reference to children is one of the reasons I believe in the inspiration of Scripture. The purpose of marriage in that culture was children, and the purpose of a woman was to bear children. Song of Songs is written as if it knew nothing of its own culture; it transcends it. Children are not necessary to justify marital love. They are not the justification of marital love; they are the expression of it. A man and a woman in love have to take precautions to keep from having children. Life is the natural expression of love, but love stands on its own feet.

I found myself interested in what this said about human sexuality. When Pope John Paul II became pope, he used the weekly chapel talks to speak about human sexuality. He spoke on human sexuality for one hundred and thirty weeks. It took him four years. He was convinced that if the Church loses the battle on sexuality, the Church will lose the battle everywhere, because this is the supreme analogy of what happens in the life of the triune God. Human sexuality and marital love are a parable of divine life and love. When that witness goes, then you get Sodom and Gomorrah.

Jeremiah continues the marital metaphor with some passages that I had never noticed. There are four passages in Jeremiah where Jeremiah speaks of cultures that lose their faith as adulterous (Jer 7:34, 16:9, 25:10, 33:10–11). The first three are all alike; they are passages where he is speaking about Jerusalem, and he is saying they are adulterous. In Song of Songs and then in the Old Testament teachings, when you see the word *adultery*, it is most often speaking of a wrong relationship between Israel and Yahweh. In the passages where Jeremiah is talking of Israel's unfaithfulness, he declared that the sign of this adultery will be the lack of the music of a wedding: "I will bring an end to the sounds of joy and gladness and to the voices of bride and bridegroom in the towns of Judah and in the streets of Jerusalem . . ." (Jer 7:34). The mark of the absence of God in Israel was the lack of the wedding song. Jeremiah 33:10–11 stated what God would do when he restored Jerusalem: ". . . there will be heard once more the sounds of joy and gladness, the voices of bride and bridegroom . . . ."

The signs of the presence of God in a society are the joyous sounds of weddings; they are the signs of the intimacy that God desires with his creation. The only hope for our society is your marriage and your relationship with your spouse. I believe it is more important than any preaching you will ever do, because the world needs some signs, and the sign that is least comprehensible to the world is the kind of love relationship that God wants to put between a man and his wife, which is the self-giving love of God. When agape love is present, people want to know where it comes from.

I think the greatest witness that I have heard in the last fifteen years is Robertson McQuilken, who was president of Colombia Bible School. I was on his mailing list when he was president of Colombia. I remember the day as clear as any day in my life. I was sitting at my desk, going through my mail, and there was a letter from Robertson McQuilken. He said,

> My dear wife, Muriel, has been in failing mental health for about eight years . . . recently it has become apparent that

Muriel is contented most of the time she is with me and almost none of the time I am away from her. It is not just "discontent." She is filled with fear—even terror—that she has lost me and always goes in search of me when I leave home . . . it is clear to me that she needs me now, full-time.

Perhaps it would help you to understand if I shared with you what I shared at the time of the announcement of my resignation in chapel. The decision was made, in a way, 42 years ago when I promised to care for Muriel "in sickness and in health . . . till death do us part." So, as I told the students and faculty, as a man of my word, integrity has something to do with it. But so does fairness. She has cared for me fully and sacrificially all these years; if I cared for her for the next 40 years I would not be out of debt. Duty, however, can be grim and stoic. But there is more; I love Muriel. She is a delight to me—her childlike dependence and confidence in me, her warm love, occasional flashes of that wit I used to relish so, her happy spirit and tough resilience in the face of her continual distressing frustration. I do not have to care for her, I get to! It is a high honor to care for so wonderful a person.[1]

With that letter, he resigned from the presidency of Colombia Bible School. That kind of love is the mark of Spirit-filled Christians, and I am convinced in our society the only person that is safe is a person who lives in and out of that divine love. We have the privilege of taking part in the divine love story that is human history, and our lives are caught up in his love.

1   McQuilken resigned from the presidency of Columbia Bible School and Seminary (now Columbia International University) in 1990.

10

Bearing the World
in Intercession

Isaiah 59:1-2; 15-16

One of the hallmarks of Papa's theology was his understanding of prayer. Relatively early in his intellectual journey, he picked up a volume by Charles Williams called *Descent of the Dove*. In this book, Williams depicts of the work of the Holy Spirit in the life of the Church. This book started Papa on an exploration of the writings of Charles Williams. One of Williams's foundational ideas was the idea of bearing one another's burdens as the key to redemption. This became the foundation for Papa's understanding of intercessory prayer. He believed that when we pray, we are not telling God something he does not already know; we express a willingness to bear the burden for those we love, and when we are willing, God has an opportunity to act.

As he did more study, Papa found that this understanding is foundational to the Hebrew text of many prophetic passages in the Old Testament, such as Isaiah 53:6. Forgiveness is not something that even God can just decree; forgiveness and redemption come when one is willing to bear another's sin. That is the essence of the cross and of what Christ willingly participated in on our behalf.

This sermon explores the ideas of divine power and intercession. God's power is not primarily in his might but in his willingness to bear our sins in himself. As we enter into intercession for others, we enter into that life of God in which we love someone else more than we love ourselves. This, for Papa, was the essence of the Good News.

> Behold the LORD's hand is not shortened, that it cannot save, or his ear dull, that it cannot hear; but your iniquities have made a separation between you and your God, and your sins have hidden his face from you so that he does not hear. . . . The LORD saw it, and it displeased him that there was no justice. He saw that there was no man, and wondered that there was no one to intercede; then his own arm brought him salvation, and his righteousness upheld him" (Isaiah 59:1–2, 15–16 ESV)

One of the proofs of the inspiration of Scripture is its interconnectedness. Sometimes, when I am reading, I find that I begin to unravel a biblical thread that runs through an entire set of books or through the entire canon of Scripture. The most impressive example of this happened in regards to a passage I was reading in Isaiah on the Lord looking for a person to stand in-between God and his world. As I read the passage, I was intrigued and began to cross reference other passages that bore this same theme of intercession. The wonder of it still amazes me.

The first of these five passages of Scripture that unpacks this biblical theme is found in Isaiah; two more are in Isaiah, one is in Jeremiah, and one is in Ezekiel. The first is Isaiah 50:1–3:

> This is what the LORD says: "Where is your mother's certificate of divorce with which I sent her away? Or to which of my creditors did I sell you? Because of your sins you were sold; because of your transgressions your mother was sent away. When I came, why was there no one? When I called, why was there no one to answer? Was my arm too short to deliver you? Do I lack the strength to rescue you? By a mere rebuke, I dry up the sea, I turn rivers into a desert; their fish rot for lack of water and die of thirst. I clothe the heavens with darkness and make sackcloth its covering."

God speaks and declares to his people that he alone is the sovereign God. His voice utters a word, and the seas dry up. He opens his mouth, and the Sahara Desert runs with water. His power is unlimited. God says to his people that their sins, not a lack of his power, are the problem. When he came to talk with them about their transgressions, he could not find even one person to respond. You will notice the way he says it, "When I came, why was there no one? When I called, why was there no one to answer?" God is perplexed (if our God can be perplexed). Where else would his people turn? Who else has the power needed to save them? No one.

Isaiah 59 reiterates this theme in a very familiar passage: "Surely the arm of the LORD is not too short to save, nor his ear too dull to hear. But your iniquities have separated you from your God; your sins have hidden his face from you, so that he will not hear" (Isa 59:1–2). God is saying to his people that there is nothing wrong with his power, there is nothing wrong with his hearing, and there is nothing wrong with his heart. If his people will turn to him, he has the power and the will to save. He is simply awaiting the opportunity. Nothing is wrong with God; the problem is in God's people. The following passage gives the most graphic picture in the Old Testament of the consequences of evil. I am sure that Nietzsche borrowed his line about a society having to light the lanterns at noon from this passage. Isaiah 59 gives a picture of a darkness so deep that lights must be turned up to full power at noon. The people of God had utterly turned away from the light of the world. The latter part of verse 15 continues the description of dark: "The LORD looked and was displeased that there was no justice. He saw that there was no one, he was appalled that there was no one to intervene; so his own arm achieved salvation for him, and his own righteousness sustained him" (Isa 59:15–16).

Each of these passages describes the *arm of the Lord*. God's own arm works salvation for him, and his own righteousness sustains him. He put on righteousness as his breastplate, the helmet of salvation on his head, and the garments of vengeance and wrapped himself in zeal as in a cloak.

Jeremiah continues the theme of the *arm of the Lord* in Chapter 5. God is speaking to Jeremiah about the city of Jerusalem and the people of God. I used to teach Hebrew, and one of the things I found in the Jewish lore was that the Jewish priests called Jerusalem "the belly button of the earth." Jerusalem is the place where heaven's umbilical cord hooks on to creation and hooks on to mankind—particularly Mount Zion, the site of God's temple. In this passage, God is talking about this most sacred earthly spot, the best the world has because of his presence. If we do not understand the significance of Jerusalem for salvation history, we will miss the significance of this passage. God is not talking about Babylon, nor is he talking about Egypt or Rome. He is talking of his own Jerusalem: "Go up and down the streets of Jerusalem, look around and consider, search through her squares. If you can find but one person who deals honestly and seeks the truth, I will forgive this city" (Jer 5:1). This verse is astonishing in terms of the potential for one person—one righteous person—to bring God's forgiveness to a whole city. It is tragic because God's people are completely separated from him.

The fifth passage about God looking for one person comes in another of the major prophets, Ezekiel: "I looked for someone among them who would build up the wall and stand before me in the gap on behalf of the land so I would not have to destroy it, but I found no one" (Ezek 22:30). God is searching for a human person. God concludes that if he could have found just one person, he would not have to act in judgment upon his people and upon his world.

After I found those verses and began to fit them together, I found my heart responding to the challenge found in them. I like the notion that one person can make a difference. Something in every person made in the image of God senses, "I ought to count." I don't believe that it is a false pride in a person that produces this aspiration and hope. We were made to count for something worthwhile. Each human person has an eternal soul; each one is made in the image of an eternal God. Of course our lives ought to count! God declares in these passages that one person does count; one person could have saved a city. I believe one person can make a difference. In fact, I suspect that every good story in human history starts with one person, and most of those whom God uses are the unlikely ones.

As I pondered these passages, I realized a second thing, which was a bit harder for me to comprehend: God *needs* one person. There is nothing wrong with God's arm, which is a symbol for his power. There is nothing wrong with God's ears; he can hear the cries of his people. There is nothing wrong with God's heart: "For God so loved the world . . ." (Jn 3:16). When he acts in judgment, it will be because he has no other option. God needs one person so he doesn't have to act in judgment. This does not fit our normal theology, but I dare you to look at the biblical text, at the truth he has given to us. In Scripture, God declares that if he could have found one person, his circumstances would have been different. Believers are quick to say that God can change our circumstances, but it is a terrifying responsibility to think that we can change God's circumstances. This idea shook me enough that it took me a while before I could go to the next step in my Bible study. I had to meditate on what it meant when Jeremiah said that if God could have found one person, he could have forgiven Jerusalem. If God had found one person, in what way would God's circumstances have been different? They would have been different in that it would have enabled God to act in mercy instead of in judgment. In every case, the options are either judgment or mercy. I do not have to explain to you what the judgment of God is. If you read the fifty-ninth chapter of Isaiah, his judgment is clear.

There is one final passage in chapter 63 of Isaiah. A conversation takes place between Isaiah and God:

> *Who is this coming from Edom, from Bozrah, with his garments stained crimson? Who is this, robed in splendor, striding forward in the greatness of his strength?*
> **"It is I, proclaiming victory, mighty to save."**
> *Why are your garments red, like those of one treading the winepress?*
> **"I have trodden the winepress alone; from the nations no one was with me. I trampled them in my anger and I trod them down in my wrath; their**

blood spattered my garments, and I stained all my clothing. It was for me the day of vengeance; the year for me to redeem had come. I looked, but there was no one to help, I was appalled that no one gave support; so my own arm achieved salvation for me." (Isaiah 63:1–5 emphasis mine)

I simply want to say: one person can make a difference. One person can actually change God's circumstances and make it possible for God to act in mercy and in redemption instead of in judgment.

People do not change easily. I have decided that not even God has an easy time transforming people's hearts. I used to think it was just me. I knew if my wife, Elsie, would listen to me for ten minutes, I could straighten her out. I tried it several times with a magnificent lack of success. It is not easy to get people to change. I found myself with five kids and sixteen grandchildren and eventually more than thirty great-grandchildren. How do I get them to change? How do I get them to come to the place where Jesus Christ is the passion of their hearts? I cannot force them or persuade them or buy them. Even God cannot force people to change. If he could, the cross would not have been necessary. That is the reason he declared that there is nothing wrong with his arm. He has all the power to change everybody in the world, but how does he get them to change? He does not sit on his throne and zap them, transforming them into holy people by eliminating their freedom.

At this point in my spiritual query, as I wrestled with this new thought, I raised a further question: "If he is looking for one person, and one person can make God's circumstances different, what kind of a person is he looking for?" I found myself wanting to be that person. Something in Isaiah 59:16 intrigued me. Most translations say, "He saw there was no one, he was appalled that there was no one to intervene." The word means "an intercessor." I grew even more curious. What kind of person is he looking for? He is looking for an intercessor. What is an intercessor? I was reading through this passage in the Hebrew and realized the word for "appalled" is actually the word for "astonished." How can the all-knowing One be surprised? Or how can Omniscience be astonished? Yet God said, "I looked, and I was astonished that I couldn't find one person."

The word for intercessor here is *maphgia*. In Hebrew, at least eighty-five percent of the words are based on what are called tri-consonantal roots, three letters that have a basic idea in them, a picture behind them. The root of this word in this passage is *pgh*. The Hebrew verb is *pg'* and it means "to meet." You put the *m* in front of it, and it means "a person," and the *a* after it means "who causes." An intercessor is one "who causes to meet." God looks for one person who can cause God—in his holiness, power, and love—to meet the world—in its sin, lostness, and blindness. He looks for one who can cause those in the trauma of sin (sin always brings trauma) to meet God in his lovingkindness and salvation.

The word *paga'* does not occur a great many times in the Old Testament, but it occurs twice in chapter 53 of Isaiah, and so I continued chasing my thread and began reading Isaiah 53. The chapter starts, "Who has believed our message and to whom has the arm of the LORD been revealed?" For the rest of Isaiah 53, he talks about the arm of the Lord. The third reference, in Isaiah 53:6, gripped me: "All we like sheep have gone astray; we have turned—every one—to his own way; and the LORD has laid on him the iniquity of us all" (ESV). The Hebrew of this verse actually says something quite different; it says, "And Yahweh has caused *to meet in* him the iniquities of us all" (emphasis mine). A light began to shine in my heart. I used to think intercession was going down my prayer list, but the intercessor God is looking for is one in whom the needs of a lost world and a holy God could meet. Intercession is not an external act but an inner condition of the heart where the lost world could meet the salvation of God.

I continued pulling at the thread, hoping to unravel more of this mystery of intercession. I noticed something in Isaiah 59. God looks for somebody to intervene, to intercede, *hiphgi'a*, and he cannot find one. He is astounded that there is no one, so his own arm brings salvation. Another light turned on in my mind. When God could not find an intercessor, what is his solution? When God could not find a person to "stand between," he became one. This is the whole story of the Incarnation.

I came from a very liberal background, where everyone was convinced that Jesus was a man and that was all. I never expected to meet a person who believed in the deity of Christ. I believe in the pre-existence of Christ. I'm an orthodox believer. I believe in the virgin birth. I believe in the resurrection. I believe in the ascension. I believe in his second return. I believe there is an uncrossable line between the creator and the creature, never crossed except at one point—in Jesus Christ. But I want to say something clearly: salvation doesn't come from above. The Savior comes from above, but salvation comes through his incarnate life. In fact, when salvation came, it came looking so much like you and me that the religious leaders said, "Look there. He is just like one of us." It took a divine revelation for Anna and Simeon to know who he was. And when he came, when salvation came, it came through his life. Salvation does not take place on the throne; it took place on a hill outside of Jerusalem in the embodiment of the arm of the Lord, the eternal Son who became one of us. Salvation cannot be handed down. We Americans would like to go to the world and hand it down to everybody in the world. We who are saved would like to hand it down to these poor, miserable, lost people, but salvation is never handed down. It goes through another life. When God could not find one, he became one.

What did God do when he became an intercessor? He bore us in his heart and in his body. The strongest word in the Old Testament for "forgive" is the word that normally is translated "to bear," which means that the word creates translation problems for scholars. Psalm 32:1 is a good example, "Blessed is the one whose transgressions are forgiven, whose sins are covered." The Hebrew for "forgiven," *naśa*, is a passive particle of the verb, "to bear." "Blessed is the man whose transgressions are borne." Somebody else has taken them. That is exactly what Christ did. He took our need. He took our sins. He took our estate. He took our circumstances. He took us into himself. And all of us met the life of God in him and were transformed. My deadness met his life.

I want to raise a question: Do you know where people come from? They come because a mother bears them in her body, and if somebody does not bear you, you will never be born. That word, *naśa'*, can be translated just exactly that way. Paul said to the Galatians, "My dear children, for whom I am again in the pains of childbirth until Christ is formed in you" (Gal 4:19). He bore those Galatians in his soul. How do you think David Livingston opened up Africa? I don't believe it was with his feet, and I don't believe it was with his mouth; I think it was in his heart. I don't think it's an accident that when the English came to get David Livingston, the Africans said, "You can have his body, but you're not going to get his heart, because his heart belongs to us." It was in the heart of David Livingstone that the liberation of Africa started. He bore that continent in his soul, and in that bearing, something began to happen in a land that had never heard the gospel.

Who are you bearing in your heart? Nobody can change on his own. The doctrine of original sin teaches that we are dead in our trespasses and sins. If we have a good thought, it did not originate with us. All goodness comes from God. All love comes from God. If I ever have a loving emotion, it does not come from me. We are dead in our trespasses and our sins. How do you get a dead person to come alive? It is not easy, because it always starts in somebody else.

I am convinced that the key to change in any human being rests in someone else's hands. The key to you is in somebody else. The key to me is in somebody else. Nobody ever starts on their own. Forget about American individualism. The redemption of the world did not start with the world; it started in the heart of the God who sent Jesus to Calvary. There would not be a chance for any of us if salvation had not started in the heart of the Father and was worked out in the body and heart and life of the Son. Through his life, our life came. He looks at you and me and says, "As the Father has sent me, I am sending you" (Jn 20:21). The key to every person rests in somebody else, and the key to somebody rests inside you. That brings me to this: before anyone else can change, we have to change. Before God asks me to change, he changed! That transforms the relationship between the saved and the lost, doesn't it? We are not called to straighten the world out but to let God straighten us out so he can reach his world. Evangelism and mission must start in our hearts; our hearts must be a place where God and the world can meet.

He is the eternal One and does not change, and yet I know that the God who rested in Mary's arms had very different circumstances from the God who sits on the throne. I ran across a verse from a Wesley hymn that I had never noticed before, a Christmas one: "Our God ever blest with oxen doth rest"—this is not the place where one could expect to find the eternal God—"Is nursed by His creature and hangs at the breast" (Charles Wesley. *Hymns for the Nativity of our Lord* (London: William Strahan, 1745), number 16). All of creation rests on this Son, and then he submits to being dependent on one of us. The potential for change in us starts in the heart of God. This should not surprise us, because it is the way interpersonal relationships work. That helped me understand something that I had wrestled with for years. Did you ever wonder why God needs to pray? I went to a friend of mine one day and said, "Why does God need to pray?"

He said, "God doesn't need to pray, we're the ones who need to pray."

I said, "Well, that's not what my Bible says."

He said, "What do you mean?"

"Well," I said, "Romans 8:26 says the Spirit intercedes for us. I think that is prayer. 'The Spirit himself intercedes for us through wordless groans.' Why does the Spirit of God need to pray for me? That verse in Romans 8 and then again in Hebrews 7:25, 'He [the Christ] ever lives to make intercession for them.' That is what he is doing at the right hand of the Father now. He, the eternal Son, prays for you and for me. I used to think that was the Son of Mary. I do not believe that any more."

When I pushed my friend, he said, "That passage in Romans is about the Son, who is interceding with the Father for us."

I said, "Well, let me ask you, is he telling the Father something he doesn't know?" He didn't like that, so I said, "Is he twisting his arm to get the Father to do something he doesn't want to do?" And my friend liked that even less.

I came to the conclusion that when your need becomes greater to me than my need, there is a possibility of your changing. That takes involvement, identification, and concern. You cannot be involved with people in this way and keep your hands clean. There is a mystery in human personhood, and if you want one person to change, somebody else has got to open the door for the possibility by taking his need into himself. When your need becomes more important to me than my own need, than your possibilities can change.

All of this is based on the nature of the Trinity. To be a person means you are incomplete. Even a perfect person would be incomplete because to be a person is to be, by definition, incomplete. We are made for someone beyond ourselves. Even a divine person is incomplete because Jesus said, "By myself I can do nothing . . ." (Jn 5:30). He said, "For as the Father has life in himself, so he has granted the Son also to have life in himself" (Jn 5:26). Do you notice that the life of the Son comes out of the Father, and our life comes out of the Son, and the life of the world comes out of us? That is the reason God starts with us. How can it be that the life of the world will come out of us? If we are what we ought to be, his life is in us.

It is interesting to think about the verses in the Bible that I was not able to look at for forty years. Philip said to Jesus, "Lord, show us the Father and that will be enough for us" (Jn 14:8). And Jesus answered, "Anyone who has seen me has seen the Father. How can you say, 'Show us the Father'? Don't you believe that I am in the Father, and that the Father is in me?" (Jn 14:9–10). I came to that verse and found that I was enamored with it, but the next part terrified me. Jesus said, "If they receive you, they get me, and when they get me, they get the Father, and if they miss you, reject you, they miss me, and when they miss me, they miss the Father. Because as the Father is in me and I'm in the Father, I'm in you and you're in me, and you're the key to the world. As I am the key to you, you're the key to the world."

Let me give you a story. The women in my life have introduced me to a British lady missionary to India by the name of Amy Carmichael. When Amy went to India, the thing that made the biggest impression on her was the state of the girls in India. She became concerned particularly about the temple girls. In India, when a husband would die, the wife would be burned on his funeral pier, because he might need her in the next life. She belonged to him; she was his possession. But when the mother was burned with the father, then what about the children? The boys were of value economically, but the girls were another story. They were a burden, so many families gave their daughters to the temple for sexual prostitution. You can imagine the disease and the trauma of those girls.

Amy Carmichael was horrified, but when she objected, the British and the Hindu communities resented her interference. Her fellow British missionaries came to Amy and said, "You're upsetting the community structure. You've got to stop rescuing these girls." In the heat of these discussions, she was working with a temple priest to get a girl out. She thought, "He's the chief priest in the temple. He's a religious man; he is bound to have some human compassion in him." So, she went and made her plea. And she said, "I could tell by the steely glint in his eye and the look on his face, he didn't have any interest in the girl. He was interested in the money she produced." Everybody seemed against Amy, and she felt completely alone.

She went back to her room and got on her face and said, "Lord, it's not my problem. I've done everything I know to do. It's not my problem." Then she saw him. He wasn't kneeling under an olive tree; he was kneeling under an Indian tamarisk tree. As she looked, she noticed he was weeping and as the tears coursed down his cheeks he looked back at her, fixed her with his eyes, and said, "You are right, Amy. It's not your problem. It's my problem. I'm just looking for somebody who'll help me bear it." Amy Carmichael went and knelt under the tamarisk tree beside her Savior. She opened her heart back to the pain, to the rejection, to the vilification, to the misunderstanding—

not only from the nationals but from her own colleagues, both secular and religious. She said, "Lord, if it's your burden, it has to be mine."

That is where the possibility of change in anybody begins, when we want to be a part of the fellowship of his suffering. Now I want to say, it isn't easy. Do you know when you've reached that point? I think you never reach it until the welfare of the other person is more important than yours. It was John Knox who said, "God, give me Scotland, or I die." It was the apostle Paul who said, "For I could wish that I myself were cursed and cut off from Christ for the sake of my people, those of my own race" (Rom 9:3). It was Moses who said, "But now, please forgive their sin—but if not, then blot me out of the book you have written" (Ex 32:32).

Dick Hillis was a Canadian missionary to China and the founder of the Formosa crusades. When he was a sixteen-year-old kid, he was out too late and he came home one night and peeped through the door into his mother's room. She was on her knees praying, and she was praying, "Lord, let me go to hell, but don't let my boy be lost." He spent his life in Christian service. I have never seen anyone change where there was not somebody else who was the key to it. It is always painful, because it always involves a cross.

I believe that God has every one of us in a place to influence the people around us. Their redemption depends on what happens right in our own hearts. The question is whether we will let God, who bears the whole world, put that concern in us. If we allow him to put his agape love into us, we will nurture the concern that comes with that love and not try to get rid of its pressures or pains. We will bear in our hearts the people God gives us.

All pregnancies are a promise. Labor is a promise, and I believe that is more true spiritually than physically. The greatest miracle is not a physical birth but a spiritual new birth. The two are analogical to each other, and so we are people who open ourselves to God to let him put within us his burden for souls in our families, our communities, our states, our nations, and even for other countries in the world. God has a burden for you to bear and a burden for me. It may be uncomfortable. It may be heavy. It may even be painful. But it will be redemptive.

Paul declared his desire in Philippians 3:10, "that I may know him and power of his resurrection, and may share his sufferings, becoming like him in his death" (ESV). How does Christ suffer after the resurrection? I believe it is the groaning for his creatures that Paul talks about in Romans 8:27, "The Spirit himself intercedes for us with groanings too deep for words" (ESV). There is pain in the heart of a Father God when he looks at a world like this. Paul wanted to enter into the suffering of Christ, and I think that has to do with the burden of intercession.

What is the burden God is putting on your heart? Have you tried to get rid of it or shuck it off? How many times, when the burden comes, do we turn our attention to something else so we do not have the responsibility or the pressure of bearing the burden? Do we have an inner witness that we are where we belong, carrying the burdens that he has assigned to us? If not, one of these days, we will know sincere regret. If we refuse the burden he is giving us, we will miss out on his blessing, our family will miss out on his blessing, our church will miss out on his blessing, and so will our nation and our world.

The beauty of the gospel is that we can enter into the burden-bearing of God himself. The Holy Spirit can give us grace to say, "Father, thank you for entrusting me with a miniscule part of your burden for this world. I may not be a very good burden bearer, but will you give me more grace so I can carry more?" The reality is that there are people under judgment who will be destroyed if someone does not intercede for them. We must embrace our burden instead of fighting it and commit ourselves to say, "Lord, I am going to keep my arms around it until delivery, because this burden is a promise of redemption in the life of someone committed to my care."

Our redemption came when God the Father bore us in his heart and Christ the Son bore us in his body. The redemption of the world will come when Christians willingly enter into that burden-bearing with Christ Jesus.

Now, be with us, Lord, and help us not to just intellectually learn this in our heads but in every fiber of our body. Let it soak down in our souls until we become burden bearers, so that Galatians 6:2 is part of our very being, "Bear one another's burdens, and so fulfill the law of Christ" (ESV).

Be with us, Lord Jesus. Amen.

CPSIA information can be obtained
at www.ICGtesting.com
Printed in the USA
BVOW06*2205120717
488513BV00005BA/7/P

9 780915 143306